MW00449925

TOTAL DESIGN

Objects by Architects

TOTAL DESIGN

Objects by Architects

DOROTHY SPENCER

CHRONICLE BOOKS   SAN FRANCISCO

This book is dedicated in loving memory to
my father, Emanuel Snyder.

Printed in Hong Kong.

Library of Congress Cataloging in Publication Data:
  Spencer, Dorothy
  Total design: objects by architects/Dorothy Spencer.
    p.   cm.
  Includes index.
  ISBN 0-87701-665-8
  1. Architect-designed furniture. 2. Architect-
designed decorative arts. I. Title.
NK2702.S6 1991   91-7133
749.2'034 — dc20   CIP

Art Direction: Jacqueline Jones
Book Design: Deborah Shubert

Distributed in Canada by Raincoast Books,
112 East Third Avenue, Vancouver, B.C., V5T 1C8

10 9 8 7 6 5 4 3 2 1

Chronicle Books
275 Fifth Street
San Francisco, California 94103

I would like to thank my mother, Edna Snyder,
and my son, Jason, for their perseverance while I
researched and wrote this book.

I would like to gratefully acknowledge the enthusiasm
and encouragement of my partner, Larry Cuba.
His belief in this project helped to make it happen.

I would also like to thank the many manufacturers
whose encouragement in this research and whose
contributions of both information and photographs have
enabled this book to come about—they are the true
instigators of total design.

Architects have been designing furniture and fixtures for their buildings for centuries. Only since the late eighteenth and early nineteenth centuries has this extension of the architectural process come to influence the entirety of the international design community.

Traditionally the structure of a building—walls, doors, windows, and other elements that create space—was designed by the architect, whereas the furniture, fabrics, and interior colors came later as an afterthought, or sometimes without any consideration of the design of the building. But for a variety of reasons that began with the birth of the Arts and Crafts Movement in response to the industrial revolution,* more and more architects started to become involved in industrial design rather than stop at the design of a building's shell. Instead of leaving the interiors to be decorated by others, architects chose to exercise control over how built space would look.

* Bauhaus manifesto

In the keynote address at the American Craft Council national conference in 1986, historian Spiro Kostof stated: " . . . A bungalow and a Gropius house, the Arts and Crafts mentality and the Bauhaus, archenemies allegedly, come together. They both insist on a total design, a consistent, custom-made world. A chair and a building are supposed to be made the same way out of a rational application of universal design principles, and built-in furniture, an aspect of the Arts and Crafts aesthetic and of Wright's practice, is also what determines Bauhaus kitchens or sleeping alcoves."

The designers in *Total Design* are all linked by a common approach. Plan and section, furniture and materials are viewed as equal partners in conveying an idea. The objects they have created are perceived as playing a major role in defining space, and the design of these objects is approached architecturally.

As architect/designer Warren Platner points out: "It is both fascinating and worthwhile to pay attention to a very simple object. Where does architecture end? Where does space end? The objects in space modify the space and have a lot to do with the success of it. So the success of the object is important, too. We ought to conceive of the building from the inside out."

In *Total Design*, architect/designers of the past 150 years who immersed themselves in all aspects of design—exterior and interior space, housewares, lighting, graphics, and the symbolic and psychological implications of color, material, and scale—are examined in the context of the period in which they practiced their art.

This history of total design provides a time line of innovators who have changed not only how we live but also how we perceive the world in which we live. By learning from the past and implementing this knowledge, these designers have provided a legacy on which future generations will build.

THE BEGINNINGS

In Great Britain during the first half of the nineteenth century, concern was expressed over the low standards of design in the decorative arts. These low standards were blamed on the rapid rise in industrialization, which emphasized quantity at the expense of quality. And, in turn, the decline in manufacturing standards was attributed to a decline in design standards resulting from inadequate educational facilities.

English architect Augustus W. N. Pugin, an early critic of design standards, believed that "a nation's art was a symptom of its moral health." Pugin was a strong supporter of the Gothic Revival style and, through his writings and speaking engagements, encouraged his colleagues as well as the public to return to the English medieval philosophy of design. Pugin's goal was to reunite art and labor, designer and craftsman, and the spiritual with the everyday.

Pugin's Gothic designs manifested more than style. They also symbolized the social structure of the Middle Ages, which for him was a period in architecture and design that had produced "stable, honest and good" products. Because of the religious associations of the Gothic period, Pugin's buildings were regarded as "spiritually and morally uplifting," especially in contrast to the grim industrial buildings in Great Britain in the middle to late nineteenth century. His furniture and wallpaper designs were stylizations from nature, including fleur-de-lis and other patterns from the Middle Ages.

Pugin's ideas on design were ahead of their time and were not completely understood by many of his colleagues. It wasn't until the middle of the nineteenth century that Pugin's views and his revival of Gothic styles were first echoed through the work of critic John Ruskin. Later in the century, they were emulated by architect William Burges before being taken up by William Morris. Through the influence of these architects, the seeds had been sown for an international design reformation known as the Arts and Crafts Movement. Its tenets would be felt in design through the middle of the twentieth century.

JOSEF HOFFMANN:
FLEDERMAUS CHAIR,
1905

CHRISTOPHER DRESSER:
PITCHER FOR LINTHORPE POTTERY

CHRISTOPHER DRESSER:
PAIR OF VASES FOR LINTHORPE POTTERY

These vases, created by Christopher Dresser in the final quarter of the nineteenth century, reveal his predilection for Japanese forms and motifs. Interest in eastern design spread to all proponents of the Arts and Crafts Movement.

THE ARTS AND CRAFTS MOVEMENT IN ENGLAND

John Ruskin, considered to be the most influential architecture critic of the nineteenth century, shared Pugin's dislike for Classical design. Ruskin believed Gothic architecture to be superior—its asymmetry and irregularity and the naturalness of its ornamentation allowed the craftsman freedom of expression.

Unlike most of the early Arts and Crafts reformers, Ruskin rejected the use of machinery. He believed that factory work had disturbed the natural rhythms of life, that it turned once-creative craftsmen into mere cogs in the machinery of industrialization, so that they, like their products, lost uniqueness. For Ruskin, the industrial revolution made designers become anonymous laborers. Only by returning to handwork would individuality and quality be restored.[1]

In 1856, architect Owen Jones published his famous *Grammar of Ornament*. Illustrated with color lithographs, it was to become the bible for ornamental styles ranging from the most primitive to the most complex mosaic designs of the Alhambra. The book also contained Jones's views on design, many of which were highly derivative of Pugin's theories and were to be echoed by members of the Arts and Crafts Movement.

"As architecture," Jones wrote, "so all works of the Decorative Arts should possess fitness, proportion, harmony, the result to which is repose. . . . Construction should be decorated. Decoration should never be purposely constructed."

One of Jones's most gifted followers was noted designer Christopher Dresser, who became a major influence on architect/designers Edward William Godwin and William Burges, predecessors of the Arts and Crafts Movement. Dresser, known for his innovative furniture, glass, and ceramic designs, was influenced by the first wave of Japanese styles that had become part of the European design vocabulary in the mid-1860s. His work also reflected many characteristics and elements of Egyptian, Greek, and Islamic art.

Like Dresser, architect/designers E. W. Godwin and William Burges began their careers as Gothic Revivalists. Even Ruskin praised much of Godwin's early architecture. By the late 1860s, the work of Godwin and Burges began to reflect a stylistic

eclecticism prefiguring that of Post-Modernism. In fact, contemporary architectural historians consider Dresser, Godwin, and Burges to be pioneers of the Post-Modernist philosophy of the 1980s.

Some of Godwin's furniture designs reveal elements of Gothic style. Others show an interest in Turkish latticework. Still others reflect Chinese sources. Godwin also produced "Anglo-Japanese" furniture while working with James McNeill Whistler.

The arts of Japan were important influences not only on Godwin's work but also on the Arts and Crafts Movement as a whole. The asymmetrical and stylized surface decoration in Godwin's work was adapted by many designers. Japanese design influenced architects from Paris, France, to Pasadena, California, and was echoed repeatedly through subsequent decades of design and a multitude of styles.

Sources as diverse as Egyptian, Greek, Chinese, Japanese, Old English, and Jacobean all appeared in Godwin's furniture. Not until the nine different chair designs produced in the 1980s by architect Robert Venturi for Knoll International can eclecticism be seen to the same extent that it was in Godwin's work.

John Ruskin's influence on design during the latter half of the nineteenth century was perhaps felt the most by William Morris, an Oxford undergraduate who gave up his early desire to enter the Church to become an architect.

In 1855, Morris began his first job, as an architect in the London office of Gothic Revivalist G. E. Street. Shortly thereafter, the Arts and Crafts Movement was born. Unable to obtain the decorative arts that he felt he needed to furnish his new home, in 1861 Morris established his own firm, Morris, Marshall, Faulkner & Co. Morris quickly abandoned his vocation of architect to become a designer of textiles, wallpaper, stained glass, and, later, books.

By 1875, the name of the company had changed to Morris & Co., establishing Morris as a producer of expensive products made by craftsmen. Like his mentor Ruskin, Morris denounced the industrial production of goods and yearned for a return to the medieval system of guilds. Morris, following Ruskin's tenets,

endorsed the belief in truth to nature and advocated the moral and social aspects of medievalism.

To an admiring public as well as to the next generation of architect/designers, Morris was the embodiment of the Arts and Crafts Movement. His views did not center simply on art and design but encompassed politics, religion, and aesthetics through his highly personal form of social idealism. Morris's work was characterized by the use of natural materials—the dyes for his textiles were made only from vegetable coloring and traditional recipes. His wallpapers and textile designs were handprinted from woodblocks and were purchased by an international clientele through department stores in Europe and the United States.

Morris's belief in the medieval system of guilds led to the establishment of several craft guilds. One of these, the Century Guild, was founded in London in 1882 by architect/designer A. H. Mackmurdo and designer/illustrator Selwyn Image. Mackmurdo, the dominant force within the guild, designed many of its products, which were produced by other Century Guild members or by firms aligned with Arts and Crafts philosophies.

Mackmurdo's designs emphasized the sinuous lines of natural plant forms, abstracted flower heads, and limpid leaf motifs, all of which anticipated the elements later found in Art Nouveau. Even though Mackmurdo was considered a forerunner of Art Nouveau, he came to reject its extreme stylishness, calling it "a strange decorative disease."

Although the Century Guild lasted only six years, it produced some of the most influential designs of the last two decades of the nineteenth century, and it set an example in both its structure and its aims for like-minded designer-craftsmen to follow.[2]

Another guild, the Art Workers' Guild, founded in 1884 in London, still exists. Its aims were "to advance education in all the visual arts and crafts, by means of lectures, meetings, demonstrations, discussions and other methods; and to foster and maintain high standards of design and craftsmanship . . . in any way which may be beneficial to the community."

Members included William Morris; architect/designer Richard Norman Shaw; William Lethaby, who, through his involvement with art education, enabled the goals of the Arts and Crafts Movement to be carried into the twentieth century;

CHARLES VOYSEY:
WRITING DESK AND
CHAIR,1896 AND 1909

This oak desk and chair
feature Voysey's
distinctive ornamental
detailing and show his
dedication to superb
craftsmanship. The chair
is one of eight created
for the offices of the
Essex and Suffolk
Equitable Insurance
Company — the
embossed monogram on
the leather back of the
chair is the company's
initials, ESI.

architect/designer Sir Edwin Lutyens; and architects C. F. A. Voysey and Charles Ashbee.

Other guilds soon sprang up in England, elsewhere in Europe, and in the United States. The Arts and Crafts Movement had important international repercussions not only as a new impetus for quality design but also as a model for craft guilds and design schools. England and the United States affected each other's Arts and Crafts movements in significant ways.

Charles Voysey was a consummate Arts and Crafts architect/designer who believed simplicity of design to be morally superior to the complexities of prior ornamentation styles. Publicly expressing disdain for shoddy craftsmanship, Voysey applied this belief in expert craftsmanship to his designs for furniture, wallpaper, and carpets. His work was often seen in publications in Europe and the United States, and by the turn of the century, his most famous designs for wallpapers and carpets were being mass-produced.

As part of the second generation of the Arts and Crafts Movement, Voysey remained loyal to the founding principles but retained few Gothic characteristics in his work. He did, however, incorporate native woods and as decoration in his furniture often used the forms created by the actual construction of the objects. He even designed hinges for some of his pieces, forming elegant strap plates similar to those on medieval furniture. Voysey also included cutouts and stylized flower heads in his chair backs. Some of his furniture had subtle hints of the Japanese influence affecting many designers of the period.

Designer Charles Robert Ashbee, another Morris disciple, founded the Guild of Handicrafts in 1888. Many of its members came from the School of Handicrafts, which he had established the prior year. Ashbee's group specialized in metalwork and jewelry, with Ashbee providing most of the designs. Ashbee, like many of his contemporaries, recognized the need for commercial retail outlets if designers and craftsmen were to survive. For that reason, guild members allowed their products to be sold in such shops as Liberty & Co. in London and, later, Tiffany's in New York.

WILLIAM MORRIS:
THE MORRIS
ADJUSTABLE CHAIR, 1865
OAK AND UPHOLSTERY
38 1/4" X 26 3/4" X 24 5/8"

HECTOR GUIMARD:
DESK, C. 1903
AFRICAN AND OLIVE ASH

Guimard's personal
interpretation of Art
Nouveau included
combining deliberate
and emphatic
asymmetry with subtle,
abstract organic carvings
and his signature
whiplash design.

ART NOUVEAU AND ITS COUNTERPARTS

While the Arts and Crafts Movement was at its height of popularity in England—a generation before its counterpart in the United States—another style of design was evolving on the European continent. Art Nouveau was a hybrid of the botanical forms found in much of nineteenth century design, including the designs of Arts and Crafts architect/designers and the imagery of Pre-Raphaelite painters. This all-embracing style found expression on every scale, from architecture to jewelry.

Art Nouveau derived from the Gothic belief in the use of ornament as a basic requirement of design. Largely a curvilinear style employing whiplash curves and flower-and-plant-based motifs, Art Nouveau displayed an ease and flair lacking in the Arts and Crafts Movement in England. Art Nouveau extolled the same Arts and Crafts beliefs in the use of expensive materials, attention to detail and craftsmanship, and love of asymmetry and sinuous curved line. It continued to influence the rest of the world through the outbreak of World War I, long after the Arts and Crafts Movement in England had declined.

The Art Nouveau hailed in France went by other names in other countries. In Italy it was called Stile Liberty; in Germany, Jugendstil; and in Vienna, Sezessionism. The influence of Japonism, with its strong emphasis on graphic forms, awareness of line, and use of woodblocklike poster prints with solid masses of color, can be seen throughout the work of European Art Nouveau architect/designers. Art Nouveau objects, like those produced by the Arts and Crafts Movement, were limited editions, expensive, and available only in specialty shops.

In Belgium, Vienna, and Germany, various progressive design movements soon went beyond the Art Nouveau style and attempted to solve the problems of design in an age that saw the beginnings of mass production and other technological advancements. Hard-line members of the English Arts and Crafts Movement refused to recognize the inevitable—the onslaught of mass production—continuing, instead, to encourage individual craftsmanship and limited-edition production methods.

In France from the 1890s through the early 1900s, Art Nouveau was the main style of artistic expression. Designers innovatively applied the highly decorative uses of color, form, and ornament to a wide range of products. Besides glassware, furnishings, and jewelry, the Art Nouveau style was translated into complex, sinuous ornamental facades of buildings with fixtures and architectural fittings that incorporated glass, copper, and ironwork.

In 1895, Samuel Bing opened L'Art Nouveau shop in Paris, where paintings, interior schemes, and furnishings were exhibited. Bing's shop became an important meeting place for craftsmen, architects, and designers who came to see exhibits of products from all over the Continent.

One of France's most famous Art Nouveau architect/designers was Hector Guimard, who in 1900 created the innovative cast ironwork for the Paris Metro stations. The entrances, banisters, and accompanying fittings all illustrate the designer's organically inspired forms and abstracted details.

Guimard, known for his belief in total design, created complete schemes for his buildings, down to such details as fireplace and light fixtures. His architectural plans, furniture, interiors, graphics, and other designs transformed the idea of organic form into a truly sculptural exercise. His style, like that of many of the Art Nouveau designers, was eclectic and borrowed from such diverse sources as Japonisme, Rococo, and Gothic.

By 1900, Art Nouveau was flourishing in Germany, Austria, Italy, France, and Belgium. In 1898, Belgian architect Victor Horta designed his Brussels home in the Art Nouveau style, to the astonishment of the architecture and design communities throughout Europe. Inspired by Art Nouveau graphic design and painting, the building was without architectural precedent. Although the plan and facade of the house were distinctive, it was the interior, with its flamboyant use of metal structure for decoration and its lush, sensuous lines, that introduced a new sense of design to the world. Horta was noted for applying, with great conviction, two of the major underlying principles of the movement: the study of nature and the notion of truth to materials.

One of the most important contributors to the development of the Art Nouveau style in Belgium and throughout the Continent was Belgian architect/designer Henry van de Velde. A strong believer in the philosophy expounded by

the Arts and Crafts Movement, van de Velde encouraged other designers to unite art and industry for the benefit of all people.

In 1895–96, commissioned by Samuel Bing, van de Velde designed four interiors for the opening exhibition at L'Art Nouveau shop, which incorporated his special language of form using abstract curvilinear shapes.

He also designed numerous buildings and interiors, and a broad range of decorative arts, from furnishings to jewelry to metalwork and light fixtures, all illustrating his unique Art Nouveau style of intense, rhythmic, curvilinear forms.

At the same time, in Barcelona, architect Antonio Gaudí interpreted Art Nouveau with a distinctiveness and individuality absent even in the designs of Horta. Although primarily an architect, Gaudí also designed furniture and metalwork, usually for his own buildings. Gaudí has been compared with his contemporary, Scottish architect/designer Charles Rennie Mackintosh; both men were regarded as maverick geniuses working at the periphery of mainstream events.

Jugendstil was developing simultaneously in Germany. In 1896, van de Velde was invited to lecture there, and in the following year, at the "Decorative Arts Exhibition" in Dresden, he exhibited the interiors he had designed for Samuel Bing's L'Art Nouveau opening. Shortly after, van de Velde took up permanent residency in Germany. His presence and the Dresden show provided a major impetus for the shaping of German Art Nouveau.

Inspired by the English Arts and Crafts Movement, several artists' colonies and workshops were soon established in Germany. Under the patronage of Grand Duke Ernst Ludwig von Hesse, an artists' colony was founded in Darmstadt in 1897. Austrian architect/designer Joseph Maria Olbrich was hired to design most of the houses for the colony, which is considered to be the high point of the German Arts and Crafts Movement. Darmstadt achieved an artistic importance far beyond the original intentions of its founder. It became the center for the creative exchanges that characterized the Arts and Crafts Movement.

Peter Behrens, a well-known Art Nouveau graphic designer, met Olbrich at Darmstadt and immediately began a

OTTO WAGNER:
ARMCHAIR, 1900-1906
CURVED WOOD

Wagner's design for
this residential seating
features little ornament
and simple lines.

new career as an architect. The artists' colony provided both Behrens and Olbrich with architectural work. Behrens was to become the most important industrial designer of his generation.

Art Nouveau in Austria, which was quite different from the style in other countries, consisted of simplified, repeating geometric shapes, such as small circles and squares, along with patterns created by severe, linear, two-dimensional planes and surfaces. Many of the designs of Viennese Art Nouveau more closely resembled those produced by the English Arts and Crafts Movement than they did Art Nouveau styles of other countries.

In a revolt against academic establishments, Austrian avant-garde architects and painters, including architect Otto Wagner and a small group of his students, formed the group known as the Sezessionists. The group's main goal was to raise the level of architecture and the decorative arts to that of the fine arts such as painting and sculpture. In addition to Wagner, the group included architect/designers Josef Hoffmann, Joseph Olbrich, Koloman Moser, and painter Gustav Klimt. In 1897, they held their first joint exhibition in Vienna, which also included the work of Henry van de Velde, Auguste Rodin, Eugene Grasset, and Fernand Khnopff.

In 1898, the Sezessionists commissioned Olbrich to build a gallery for their annual exhibitions. At the same time, they began publishing a magazine, *Ver Sacrum*, which provided an important outlet for their writings and influential points of view on all areas of design.

Olbrich based his design for the Sezessionist building on a sketch by Gustav Klimt from the cover of an issue of *Ver Sacrum*. The drawing was of a building that was radically different from anything already existing in conservative Vienna. According to design historian Penny Sparke, Klimt's drawing, containing a decorated dome and severe facade, proposed a building that both defended and criticized Art Nouveau. Olbrich's building reflected the basic Sezessionist style of geometrically inspired structure and decoration.

With the completion of the Sezession building, the Sezessionists' influence was immediate and far-reaching, establishing Vienna as an international center for applied arts.

The Sezessionists took the Arts and Crafts philosophy of pure form and materials and applied it to the manufacture of

OTTO WAGNER:
TRAMWAY, 1900
CEILING LAMP
9 3/8" X 11 3/4"

OTTO WAGNER:

POST OFFICE SAVINGS BANK, 1903-1912
VIENNA, AUSTRIA

POSTAL SAVINGS STOOL, 1904
STEAM-BENT ELM LEG AND
SEAT FRAME; MOLDED
PLYWOOD SEAT
15 1/4" X 15 1/4" X 181/2"

Completed in two
phases, 1904-1906 and
1910-1912, the building
is thought to be the
masterpiece of Wagner's
late career. The architect
combined aluminum,
steel, and concrete—
new materials of the
period—with white
marble and glass bricks
to create a disciplined
and immaculately crafted
work of architecture.

CHARLES RENNIE
MACKINTOSH:
BUFFET, 1918
EBONIZED ASHWOOD
63 1/2" X 22 1/4" X 58 7/8"

In keeping with the
architect's desire for
simple yet elegant form,
the only decoration is
the colored glass mosaic
bound with lead in the
center of the buffet,
outlined with inlaid
pieces of mother-of-
pearl, all of which echo
the geometric lines of
the cabinetry.

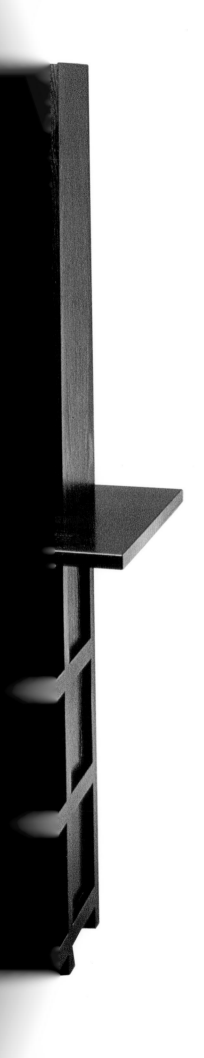

decorative arts, promoting a harmony between designers and manufacturers. They created a visual vocabulary for the applied arts that possessed clear national characteristics, yet they still viewed themselves as just one part of an international revolutionary movement in design of which John Ruskin and William Morris were "revered ideological precursors."

The most significant contributor to the development of the international Art Nouveau style was Scottish architect/designer Charles Rennie Mackintosh. Mackintosh, a major follower of Voysey, began his career in Glasgow after graduating from the Glasgow School of Art. His early work was publicized extensively in *Studio* magazine.

Mackintosh, along with his wife, Margaret Macdonald, and Herbert McNair and his wife, Frances Macdonald, formed a group known as the Glasgow Four. The group not only encapsulated Arts and Crafts and, later, Art Nouveau visions of a unity in the fine and applied arts but also evolved highly original concepts of form and decoration.

The Glasgow Four exhibited their work in London in 1890. Other exhibitions followed in France, and then, in 1900 in Vienna, the four were invited to exhibit with the Sezessionists. This cooperative effort influenced many designers abroad—particularly the Vienna Sezessionists.[3]

Mackintosh's work combined the qualities of space found in Pre-Raphaelite graphics with an architectural sense found in Arts and Crafts-based furniture design. His furniture manifested an interplay of lines created by the actual forms of the pieces interacting with elements such as geometric shapes of inlaid wood or painted geometric forms that were applied to the objects. Mackintosh's chairs often contained elongated backs with long tapering arms and legs and were decorated with pierced grids or other linear patterns or with stenciled motifs. Even his designs for cutlery and candlesticks reflected these qualities.

Mackintosh's work had greater influence in Austria and Germany than it did in England since his furniture designs were more abstract and stylized than most adherents of the Arts and Crafts Movement found acceptable. He also did not share the Arts and Crafts devotion to craftsmanship—his buildings often violated traditional methods of construction.

CHARLES RENNIE
MACKINTOSH:
LADDERBACK CHAIR, 1902
MORTISE-AND-TENON SOLID
ASHWOOD CONSTRUCTION

This chair was part of a total refurbishment of Hous'Hill, the home of one of Mackintosh's most important patrons, Miss Cranston. A pair of these chairs was made of ebonized wood to be used in one of the house's many bedrooms.

CHARLES RENNIE
MACKINTOSH:
DINING TABLE, 1918
EBONIZED ASHWOOD
FRAME
69" X 48 3/4" X 29 1/4"

This oval dining table
has a drop-leaf top with
a pedestal base
designed in the
architect's signature grid
frame.

JOSEF HOFFMANN:
FLEDERMAUS TABLE,
1905
BENTWOOD FRAME
25 3/8" X 25 3/4" DIAMETER

Hoffmann and other
members of the Wiener
Werkstätte designed the
interior and furnishings
of the Cabaret
Fledermaus in Vienna in
a proto-modern style.
This table is
representative of the
series.

One of Austria's most important architects, Josef Hoffmann, visited Mackintosh in Scotland at the turn of the century. This visit greatly influenced Hoffmann, and Mackintosh's unique style became a major inspiration in the development of Art Nouveau in Austria. At the 1902 Turin exhibition, Austrian design, with its rectilinear forms, immediately became an international success. One of the most influential exhibits for the Sezessionists was a room setting designed by Mackintosh.

The following year, in 1903, Hoffmann, with Austrian architect Koloman Moser, founded the Wiener Werkstätte, a Viennese Arts and Crafts workshop that followed English Arts and Crafts principles, influenced by the Mackintosh aesthetic. Although the objects produced at the workshop were designed with the intention of counterbalancing the proliferation of machine-produced objects, the simple geometric forms that dominated the line of products were quite similar to the shapes found in machine-made objects from Germany and the United States. But unlike the objects from Germany and the United States, the Werkstätte designs were not affordable for the general public.

During Hoffmann's reign at the Weiner Werkstätte, he created some of the most innovative and timeless designs produced during the period. The elements in his work were similar to those in Mackintosh's designs: geometric shapes combined with straight lines, contrasting black and white tones, and little surface decoration. Hoffmann used cubes and squares in much of his work and by the late 1890s was incorporating cube patterns in many of his interior schemes, from wall patterns, windows, and carpets to furnishings. An interest in the abstract motifs of Japanese design is also revealed in Hoffmann's designs, especially in his architecture and furniture.

Koloman Moser's designs reflected the linear formats found in the work of Mackintosh and Hoffmann. Moser favored black and white in a wide range of commercial designs, including book covers, metalware, textiles, wallpapers, and even bank notes.

Moser and Hoffmann followed a Functionalist approach in their innovative works, many of which anticipated the Modernism later found in Art Deco. The designs of the Weiner Werkstätte combined the characteristics of both early Modernism and the standardization of mass production while retaining the use of decoration.

The Werkstätte, although modeled after British Arts and Crafts guilds, was more versatile and achieved greater commercial success than the guilds. By 1905, it employed over one hundred craftsmen. It was equally successful in its manufacture of mass-produced, inexpensive articles as it was in the production of individually crafted, expensive objects.

With the departure of Moser from the Werkstätte in 1906, the purist style that reflected its founders began to disappear. A more decorative style took hold—one that was less avant-garde. The products were no longer viewed by the public as innovative, and by 1933 the Werkstätte was dissolved.

Because many Arts and Crafts proponents expounded a dislike for the use of machinery, the movement can be viewed as antimodern and conservative. Other observers, however, see the Arts and Crafts Movement as the crucial link between the Victorian and International styles, contributing to the Modernism of the 1920s through the principles of simplicity, abstraction, and utility and the rejection of academic styles.[4]

The ideal of the Arts and Crafts Movement was not so much one style as it was an attitude toward the making of objects. None of the separate movements in Great Britain, on the Continent, and in the United States believed in a single approach to design: each included architect/designers of varying convictions.

THE ARTS AND CRAFTS MOVEMENT IN THE UNITED STATES

By the mid-nineteenth century, the United States, like Great Britain, was striving to standardize production in order to meet the increasing demands from a mass market. American manufacturers began to mechanize the production of complex processes such as gun making, in contrast to the British, who mass-produced simple craft items such as unpatterned textiles. This difference had significant implications. The American application of industrial interchangeability and standardization quickly influenced the manufacture of such products as furniture, hardware, and ploughs and similar types of elaborate machinery. What came to be called the "American system of manufacture" helped to develop a clear demand for new high-technology products.

So strong was this drive that little time or thought was given to quality design of products. Because of the nature of mechanization, the final objects were little more than the visual result of their production and assembly processes. The quality of design for the most part remained unquestioned by consumers.[5]

When such inventions as the Colt revolver and the McCormick reaper, with their standardized, interchangeable parts, were exhibited at the 1851 "Great Exhibition" in London's Crystal Palace, many Great Britains viewed them as indicating an acceptance of the machine. Praised for their utility, these products foreshadowed the beginnings of the machine aesthetic.

GUSTAV STICKLEY:
ARMCHAIR, C. 1912

THE PHILOSOPHERS
OF ARTS AND CRAFTS

B ritish sculptor Horatio Greenough, an early proponent of Functionalist theory, took the opportunity of the "Great Exhibition" to praise American shipbuilders and engineers and warn against the "superficial, stylish excesses" of European products. In 1852, Greenough wrote the book *Form and Function*, in which he compared a ship to an animal "whose body is perfectly suited to the actions it performs and whose appearance is determined by the body's internal structure." Greenough's theories were among several influences on American architect/designers who incorporated into their own designs the philosophies of British Arts and Crafts proponents.

Although the Arts and Crafts Movement in the United States developed a generation later than its British and European counterparts, forerunners of the American movement held beliefs and working styles comparable with those of Ruskin and Morris.

English architect and furniture designer Charles Lock Eastlake, more than any other individual, was responsible for introducing English design reforms to the American public. In 1868, Eastlake wrote *Hints on Household Taste*, which inspired furniture manufacturers to produce rectilinear, Gothic-inspired furnishings. Eastlake had written the book to instruct the public in the principles of home decoration. The publication was so popular that it was reprinted four times in England and, after 1872, six times in the United States.

Hints advocated simply designed, functional furniture "honestly constructed without sham or pretense, and ornamented with respect for the intrinsic qualities of the wood as well as the intended function of the furniture." Eastlake felt that machine carving should not look like hand carving and that simplicity should be the keynote for design.

Eastlake's book gave specifics of design, construction, ornamentation, and manufacture for many other household articles, including wallpaper, metalwork, ceramics, draperies, and even clothing and jewelry.[6]

Another important event was the publication in 1862 of British designer Christopher Dresser's book *Principles of*

FRANK FURNESS:
COLUMN CAPITAL,
1873-1875
GUARANTEE TRUST
AND SAFE DEPOSIT
COMPANY, PHILADELPHIA,
PENNSYLVANIA

Incised floral patterns such as the ones on this capital were characteristic of the architect's interior styles. The bank's central opening was "choked" with columns such as these.

FRANK FURNESS:
**INTERIOR DOOR PANEL
WITH BRASS TRIM,**
GUARANTEE TRUST
AND SAFE DEPOSIT
COMPANY, PHILADELPHIA,
PENNSYLVANIA

LOUIS SULLIVAN:
**AUDITORIUM HOTEL
DINING ROOM**, C.1890

Sullivan insisted on building the dining room on the tenth floor of the Auditorium Hotel in Chicago to give the patrons a building-long view of Michigan Boulevard and the lake. The dining room contained a barrel-vaulted ceiling that sprang directly from the floor; the main dining area was separated at either end from smaller dining areas by a row of mahogany columns. The ceiling was richly stenciled in dull gold, and wide friezes of ornamental plaster surrounded by picturesque murals made the room one of the architect's finest pieces of work.

Decorative Design, which initiated rules for the construction of furniture. These are evident in the furniture designs of Philadelphia architect Frank Furness, who incorporated in many of his pieces conventionalized plant ornamentation based largely on the work of Dresser.

Furness was a major influence on architect Louis Sullivan, who had worked for Furness before moving to Chicago. Sullivan was also interested in the theories expounded in Greenough's *Form and Function*. Like Greenough, he applied "organic" architecture to his own designs. Sullivan believed that the exterior form of a building should be dictated by its interior function, which, in turn, should determine how the building in its entirety is structured.

By the late 1880s, Sullivan had started to incorporate ornament into the interiors and facades of his buildings. The roots of his beautiful floral motifs can be traced to Furness's use of conventionalized ornament. Sullivan's approach became highly individualistic, however, using strong, simple forms with complex detailing that recalled the austerity of the prairies, coupled with motifs taken from flowers, grass, and seeds. Although Sullivan was not a disciple of Morris (even though many of his followers, including Frank Lloyd Wright and George Grant Elmslie, were), he espoused a belief in an American architecture based upon freedom of expression and use of nature, unfettered by old world stylistic traditions.

American decorative arts followed in the wake of British developments. Within a decade of the founding of the various influential Arts and Crafts guilds in Great Britain in the late 1880s, arts and crafts organizations proliferated in the United States, especially in the Northeast and in Chicago and elsewhere in the Midwest. The Arts and Crafts Movement in the United States became identified with an emerging nationalism—a pride in American design and innovation that no longer relied on Great Britain and Europe for ideas. American architecture and decorative arts provided consumers with new levels of comfort and practicality. Among these sentiments was an element of nostalgia for a simpler time, which resulted in a revival of vernacular architecture and native crafts.

At the beginning of the twentieth century in the United States, the philosophy of the Arts and Crafts Movement

LOUIS SULLIVAN:
BAYARD BUILDING,1897
65 BLEEKER STREET
NEW YORK CITY

The Bayard Building
was Sullivan's first
major commission that
was executed in
independent practice. As
Robert Twombly has
pointed out in his book,
*Louis Sullivan: His Life
and Work*, Sullivan
preferred the Bayard to
all his other tall
buildings. Above the
base he placed an
elaborate arched
medallion atop the
entrance, reminiscent of
the Guarantee and the
Burnet Hotel project.

GREENE & GREENE:
WRITING DESK, C. 1908
HONDURAS MAHOGANY,
WITH FRUITWOOD INLAYS
THE DAVID B. GAMBLE
HOUSE, PASADENA,
CALIFORNIA

The dogwood motif that appears on the vase atop the writing desk recurs on the desk's pigeonhole covers. Such scrupulous attention to detail was a hallmark of Greene & Greene's work.

attracted both conservatives, who longed for the stability of the preindustrial past, and progressives such as Louis Sullivan and Frank Lloyd Wright, who believed that for designers to produce a truly democratic art they must learn not only to accept the machine but also to embrace it.

The architecture and decorative arts of the Arts and Crafts Movement in the United States, as elsewhere, cannot be described as one unifying style but manifested diverse styles created by individuals who maintained a "sometimes kindred spirit and an allegiance to creating an organic art and architecture that owed its origins to William Morris." [7] In the United States, where the geographic demands were as diverse as the geographic attitudes, many of the proponents of the Arts and Crafts Movement based their designs upon regional eccentricities, which caused the movement to have an even broader range than its British and European counterparts.

The Arts and Crafts Movement in the United States also owed a debt to such European movements as Vienna Sezession, German Jugendstil, and the Art Nouveau styles of Victor Horta and Hector Guimard. But of more importance to many American Arts and Crafts designers was the influence of the Far East— Japan in particular.

The impact of Japanese art can be seen in the work of Charles and Henry Greene of California, who early on in their careers epitomized the Arts and Crafts Movement. Their love of oriental architecture, with its emphasis on horizontal lines and simple floor plans, combined with the indigenous California shingled bungalow style, resulted in a series of homes that reflected the Arts and Crafts philosophy carried to its most uncompromised state.

The Greene brothers believed in creating a totally designed environment. They determined the needs of their client, then formulated a design concept that encompassed site, home, and furnishings. The structure of the house, its joints and motifs, was repeated in appropriate scale in each piece of furniture, rug, light fixture, and accessory.

Because of the cultural mixture of easterners, Asians, and Hispanics in California, the region's architecture and design were more of an amalgam than they were in other areas of the country. Many of the easterners who had come West

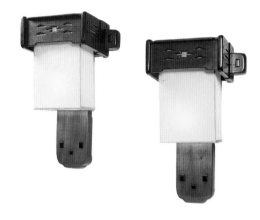

GREENE & GREENE:
PAIR OF WALL SCONCES
C. 1907-1909
MAHOGANY, EBONY PEGS,
AND GLASS 18 1/2" X
11 3/4" X 7 1/4" EACH
FROM THE DINING ROOM
OF THE ROBERT R. BLACKER
HOUSE,
PASADENA, CALIFORNIA

This pair of wall sconces was designed to provide ambient light in the dining room on the main floor of the Blacker house. Like most of the furniture designed by Greene & Greene, these fixtures were produced by the workshops of Peter Hall and Emile Lange. They are a basic T-form pierced at the top, inset with bits of colored glass, and fitted with yellow opalescent glass panels having pendant rectangular silk shades. (From *From Architecture to Object*, October 7 - November 18, 1989, Hirschl & Adler Galleries, New York, p. 116.)

GREENE & GREENE:
**ENTRANCE HALL AND
STAIRWAY**, C. 1907
THE DAVID B. GAMBLE
HOUSE, PASADENA,
CALIFORNIA

Strong verticals and
horizontals in both
architectural elements
and furnishings were
typical of the innovative
designs of Greene &
Greene. In the Gamble
House, no detail was
overlooked or left to the
whims of the owner —
the furniture, lighting
fixtures, carpets, picture
frames, even the curtain
rods, were designed to
fit into the whole
composition.

**PHOTOGRAPH OF
STICKLEY HOME AT
CRAFTSMAN FARMS,
NEW JERSEY**,
C. 1911

The caption in the 1911
issue of *The Craftsman
Magazine* reads: "This
semi-rustic home, with
its massive log walls,
shingled gables and
dormers, rough stone
chimneys and stone
kitchen, harmonizes well
with its woodland
surrounds: as some of
our readers may
remember, it is the home
of Mr. Stickley, at
Craftsman Farms, N.J. "

acknowledged the importance of the romanticism of the Franciscan missions built earlier by the Spaniards. Mission features began to appear in many architectural projects, and by the early 1900s the Mission Style of architecture and design had reached the East. Much of this was due to Gustav Stickley's rhapsodizing of the style in his magazine *The Craftsman*. Soon the term *Mission Style* was being applied not only to architecture but to furnishings as well.

San Diego based architect/designer Irving Gill interpreted the Mission Style in his architecture with a sophisticated primitivism that exemplified a direction taken by many of the American Arts and Crafts designers. Gill used advanced construction techniques such as poured concrete to build his simple cube houses.

Although the Greenes' uncompromising philosophy of design exemplified the Arts and Crafts Movement in the United States, it was Gustav Stickley who became the movement's true leader. Not formally trained as an architect, he nevertheless believed in the totally designed environment. His ideas were reflected in *The Craftsman*, a publication that fostered the ideals and goals of the Arts and Crafts Movement in the United States. Within a year after the magazine's founding in 1901, Stickley began publishing his house designs as an extension of his furniture designs.

The Craftsman was less than five years old when it attracted contributors such as Irving Gill, Charles and Henry Greene, and Grosvenor Atterbury, all of whom echoed the philosophy of Stickley's total design. Through *The Craftsman*, Stickley was able to promote the Arts and Crafts ideals to a middle class that otherwise would not have been reached. In 1911, Stickley established the Craftsman Contracting Company to build Stickley–designed homes. Craftsman houses, many of which reflected the California bungalow style, were built in almost every community in the United States.

It was Stickley's popularization of the craftsman's ideals that helped to broaden the demand for quality goods. Stickley appointed himself spokesman of "the great middle classes, possessed of moderate culture and moderate material resources, modest in schemes and action, average in all but virtue."

GUSTAV STICKLEY:
BOX SETTLE, C. 1904
OAK
29" X 76" X 32"

This settle appeared in Stickley's 1904 furniture catalogue and was available with either leather or canvas upholstery. (From *From Architecture to Object*, October 7 – November 18, 1989, Hirschl & Adler Galleries, New York.)

FRANK LLOYD WRIGHT:
**DINING TABLE WITH
EIGHT CHAIRS**, C. 1904
TABLE: OAK
28 3/4" X 60" X 54 1/2"
CHAIRS: OAK, WITH
LEATHER UPHOLSTERY

This furniture setting is
among Wright's most
famous from the Prairie
School designs.
Variations of it appear in
many of his interior
perspective drawings
from that period.

Although the ideals of the Arts and Crafts Movement promoted
purity of design and material, the products created by architect/
designers and craftsmen were usually too expensive for the
average citizen to acquire.

Although the Northeast and California nurtured diverse
styles of design within the Arts and Crafts Movement, Chicago
was one of the movement's most important centers. The midwestern movement was, in fact, closely akin to the British.

William Morris was well known to Chicagoans since his
fabrics, wallpapers, and furnishings could be purchased at local
department stores. The William Morris Society was established
in Chicago in 1903. A number of similar organizations were
founded, many of which had workshops, salesrooms, and annual
exhibitions. In addition, many influential periodicals were
published in Chicago: *House Beautiful*, *CommonClay*, *Ornamental
Iron*, *Inland Architect and News Record*, *Western Architect*, *Fine
Arts Journal*, and *Builder and Woodworker*.[8]

An early exponent of the Arts and Crafts philosophy of an
America architecture based upon freedom of expression and
nature was Louis Sullivan. He also was Frank Lloyd Wright's
employer from 1887 through 1893. Early in his career, Wright
had become a strong supporter of the movement's ideals,
extolling the virtues of Ruskin, Morris, and Japanese art and
design. In 1897, he cofounded the Chicago Arts and Crafts
Society. But unlike Ruskin, who denounced the use of machinery, Wright declared that "my god is machinery." He believed
that architecture and design in the future should incorporate the
capabilities of the machine but always under the creative
supervision of the artist.

In a 1908 article for the publication *In the Cause of
Architecture*, Wright wrote, "The most truly satisfactory apartments are those in which most or all the furniture is built in as a
part of the original scheme. The whole must always be considered as an integral unit." Wright's furniture, even those pieces
that were not designated as built-ins, were designed with specific
locations in mind since the totality of the design of a space was
carefully planned out. He called this consistency of integration
"organic design," an idea that reflected the influence of Sullivan
and Greenough.

Addressing the capabilities of the machine, Wright gave

FRANK LLOYD WRIGHT:
URN, C. 1900
REPOUSSE COPPER
18 1/2" X 18 1/2"

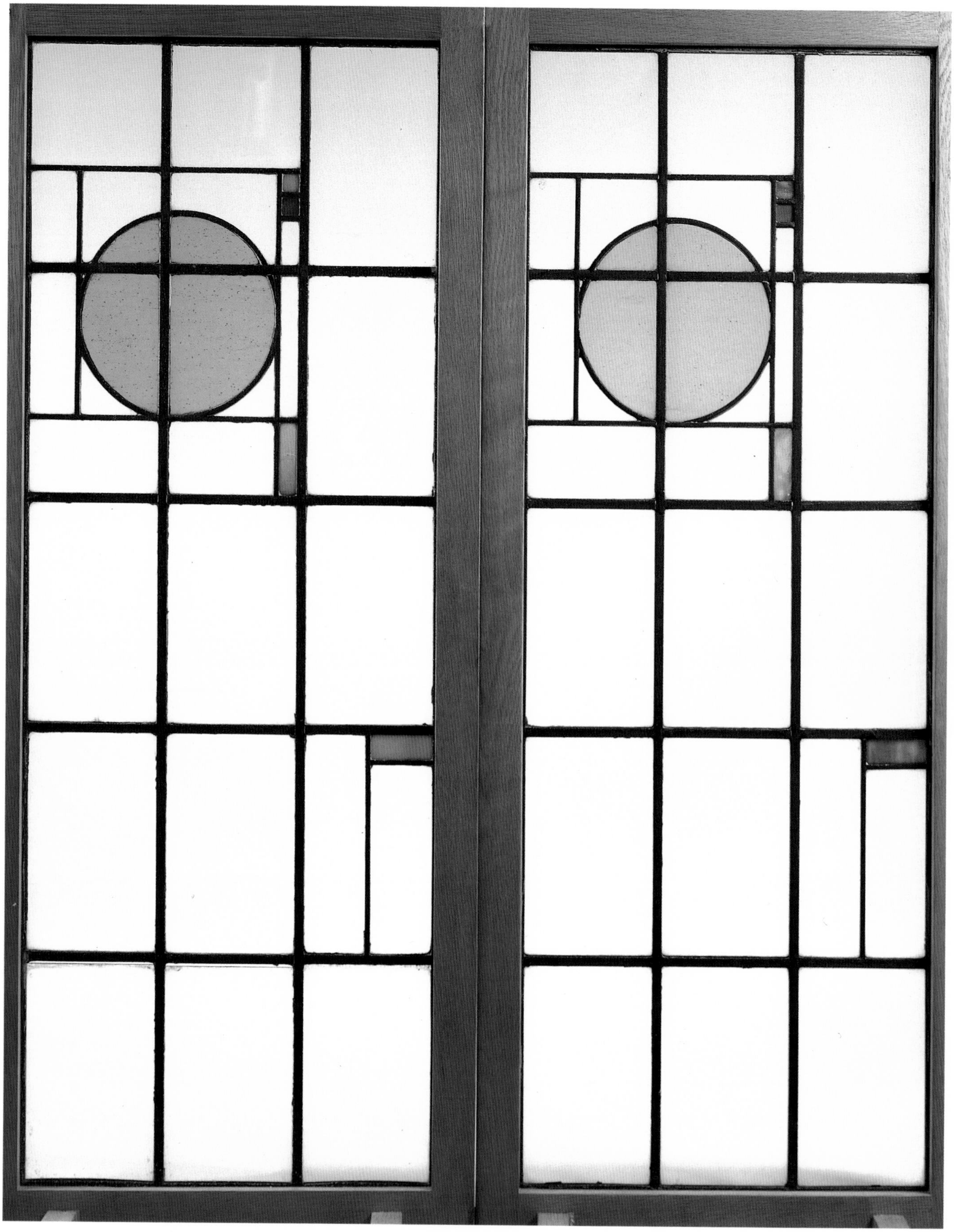

GEORGE GRANT ELMSLIE:
**PAIR OF LEADED
GLASS WINDOWS**
C. 1924
LEADED GLASS
EACH: 44 1/2" X 16 12"
FROM THE BABSON HOUSE,
RIVERSIDE, ILLINOIS

his furnishings flat, straight surfaces that lent themselves to machine production. But Wright's embrace of the machine was more ideal than practical: even his most crudely built furniture was not made entirely by machine.

At the zenith of Wright's long and prolific career, he actually lived the fable envisioned by Viennese architect Adolf Loos: Wright demanded that he be allowed to design every interior detail of his houses, right down to floor coverings and table linens. He even wanted to redesign the telephone. Wright created as many of the furnishings for his buildings as his clients were able to afford, and for those who were unable, he recommended Stickley's simple furnishings.

By the early 1900s, Wright and his associates George Grant Elmslie and George Washington Maher had arrived at what was to become known as the Prairie School of architecture. Deriving its name from the character of the midwestern countryside itself, the school was known for designs "dictated by the vast reaches of the prairie."

Elmslie's designs, like those of the other Prairie School members, were highly derivative of the Arts and Crafts Movement. Although strongly influenced by Wright, Elmslie made furniture that is less rectilinear and geometric than Wright's, due to the impact of Sullivan's flowing ornamental details.

Maher, on the other hand, was greatly influenced by modern European architecture. In a 1907 issue of *Architectural Record*, Maher explained his theory of motif rhythm in the design of his buildings and furnishings: "The fundamental principle being to receive the dominant inspiration from the patron, taking into strict account his needs, his temperament, and environment, influenced by local color and atmosphere in surrounding flora and nature."

The nature of the Arts and Crafts Movement in the United States can be seen through the success of its architectural achievements. The philosophy of a total and pure design, whether found in California bungalows, horizontal Prairie School houses, shingled and clapboard farmhouses, or Spanish Mission stucco dwellings, created a design revolution in the early part of the twentieth century. The architect/designers, though in many ways echoing the philosophies of their European counterparts, expressed their ideas in a truly American vernacular.

FRANK LLOYD WRIGHT:
TABLE LAMP C. 1902-1903
LEADED GLASS AND
BRONZE
24 1/2" X 29" DIAMETER
FROM THE SUSAN L. DANA
HOUSE, SPRINGFIELD,
ILLINOIS,

MODERNISM BEFORE THE SECOND WORLD WAR

By the turn of the century, the foundations of the international Modern movement had been laid. According to design historian Penny Sparke, mechanization, mass production, and mass consumption dictated new sets of rules for the designer, and the nineteenth century preoccupation with individualism and symbolism seemed less and less appropriate to a world increasingly dominated by the machine.

In the United States, Frank Lloyd Wright, who had founded the Chicago Arts and Crafts Society and admired Ruskin and Morris, admitted that with the growth of mass markets, "the normal tool of civilization" was the machine. To keep the cost of mass production low and to facilitate standardization, industry demanded simplicity in design.[9]

By 1914, many of the idealistic theories of architects and designers had become more directly aligned with modern practice and with the requirements of contemporary life. Their ideas owed much to their nineteenth century precursors—to the Functionalism of Pugin, Morris, and others—but were to have more far-reaching effects.[10]

In 1909 in Italy, painter and poet Filippo Marinetti published the Futurist manifesto that praised the virtues of the machine and glorified speed and movement as well as an industrialized way of life. Italian Futurists, one of the first groups of artists and writers to celebrate the power of the machine, openly challenged the antimachine tenets of Ruskin and Morris. The reverberations of the Futurist manifesto caused many Modernist designers to adopt a depersonalized approach to design.

By 1910, the Austrians and Germans began to surpass the British in the quality of practical solutions to the problems of art education, craft, design, and architecture, and in the originality of their designs. At the same time, radical Viennese architect Adolf Loos started to design buildings that to many of his contemporaries seemed alarmingly anonymous and devoid of any kind of ornament. This lack of ornament was to characterize much of twentieth-century design.

GERRIT RIETVELD:
ZIGZAG CHAIR, ORIGINAL
DATE OF DESIGN, 1934

THE DEUTSCHE
WERKBUND AND AFTER

In 1907, the Deutsche Werkbund was founded at Dresden by critic and educator Hermann Muthesius and such members as Walter Gropius, Richard Riemerschmid, and Peter Behrens. Although the group inherited its sense of reform from the British Arts and Crafts Movement, the purpose of the Werkbund was more modern: it was organized as a pressure group to encourage cooperation between art and industry.

Muthesius was concerned that there be a thorough knowledge and understanding of the processes involved in the design of mass-produced goods. This understanding would enhance the design and quality of industrial products, and in turn, the general public would come to appreciate a higher caliber of design.

A main goal of the Werkbund was to integrate the ideals of the Arts and Crafts Movement with the machine style—the clean-lined Functionalism demanded by industrialization and mass production. This achievement became a major development in the advancement of the Modern movement. Members of the Werkbund applied to their designs the basic principles of twentieth century design—Functionalism, rational construction techniques, and use of the grid. In 1911 and 1912, the designs and products of the Werkbund were exhibited in several cities throughout the United States. The influence of the Werkbund and its Modernist approach to the design and creation of industrial goods was immediate.

In 1914, the Werkbund held an exhibition in Cologne for which Walter Gropius and Adolf Meyer built the Werkbund Pavilion containing glass-enclosed helical corner stair towers and a wraparound glass corridor. Gropius quickly became the spokesman for architecture and design completely based on the machine.

The influence of the Deutsche Werkbund became international in scope. It inspired the formation of progressive design and craft schools such as the Design and Industries Association in England and the Svenska Sljödforeningen in Sweden as well as several European avant-garde art movements including Art Deco and De Stijl. Werkbund members were instrumental in the development of Modernism in all areas of

WALTER GROPIUS AND
ADOLPH MEYER:
FAGUS SHOE FACTORY,
ALFELD-AN-DER-LEINE,
GERMANY, 1910

Using classical devices
to manipulate the
building's forms, the
Fagus Shoe-Last Factory
was considered
"startlingly ahead of its
time." Especially novel
was the substitution of
steel and glass for
conventional load-
bearing walls.

design throughout the twentieth century.

In 1922, founding Werkbund member Peter Behrens wrote in *Die Form*, the Werkbund journal: "We have no choice but to make our lives more simple, more practical, more organized and wide-ranging. Only through industry have we any hope of fulfilling our aims." Behrens's career well illustrated the way in which the concerns first aired by William Morris found concrete expression in Germany in the early decades of the twentieth century. While serving as director of the School of Applied Arts in Düsseldorf in 1903 and realizing the implications of industrialization and the potential of the machine, Behrens reorganized the school's curriculum in an attempt to reconcile traditional craftsmanship and mechanized production.

The German general electricity company and one of the country's biggest concerns, the Allgemeine Elektrizitätsgesellschaft (AEG), appointed Behrens director of the company in 1907. Besides creating some of the AEG's factory buildings, including its famous turbine-construction hall in Berlin, Behrens also designed many of the company's products, which ranged from telephones to street lamps. Behrens had a private architectural practice while working at the AEG. Among the many fledgling architects who worked for him were Le Corbusier, Walter Gropius, and Mies van der Rohe.

Another Deutsche Werkbund member whose work and ideas were of importance later for the Bauhaus was Belgian architect Henry van de Velde. Van de Velde realized the dream of "cooperation between artist, craftsman and industrialist" six years before the founding of the Werkbund. In 1901, at the invitation of Grand Duke Wilhelm of Saxe-Weimar, van de Velde established an arts and crafts school where designers and craftsmen were taught to create well-designed objects for series production. Twenty years later, the Weimar school would reemerge as the Bauhaus with Walter Gropius as director.

Movements such as Vorticism in England, De Stijl in the Netherlands, Suprematism followed by Constructivism in Russia, Futurism in Italy, and Cubism in France were, like the Weimar school, already beginning to focus on geometric designs and avoid the ornate decorativeness of such styles as Art Nouveau. The geometric and abstract painting of these fine arts movements all contributed to Modernist design.

PETER BEHRENS:
THE AEG TURBINE HALL IN BERLIN, 1909

The AEG hall is Behrens's most famous building. According to design historian Stephen Bayley, it has played a seminal role in the emergence of modern architecture, demonstrating the architect's fundamental classicism.

GERRIT RIETVELD:
RED/BLUE CHAIR, 1917
34" X 25 5/8" X 33"

Rietveld's *Red/Blue Chair* is as an icon for modern life. An archetype of De Stijl design, it also stands as a three-dimensional realization of the philosophy of the De Stijl movement. This was accomplished through a very simple, yet highly sophisticated joining of colored shapes. With this, Rietveld redefines the "chair" and does so without precedent.

DE STIJL

The outbreak of World War I caused a significant interruption in the progress of innovative design styles. With the exception of certain continuing technological developments, most architecture and design work ceased. The war can be seen as a dividing line between the past and the future—a separation between a time when old-world craftsmanship was available only to the wealthy and the coming of the Machine Age when mass production would make quality products available to everyone.

During World War I, the Netherlands had remained neutral, enabling its architects, designers, and artists to continue to practice. It was in Holland, in 1917, that the De Stijl design movement was founded by Theo van Doesburg. Considered by historians to be the first major Modern design movement, De Stijl published a manifesto in 1918. It called on "all of those who believe in the reform of art and culture to destroy those things which prevent further development, just as in the new plastic art, by removing the restriction of natural forms, they have eliminated what stands in the way of the expression of pure art." In 1917, van Doesburg first published the magazine *De Stijl*, which served as a focal point for the dissemination of Modernist ideas from Europe, Russia, and the United States. De Stijl was also called Elementarism because of the emphasis on basic elements in design—horizontal and vertical lines and essential colors.

Among the founding members of De Stijl were architects Jan Wils, Robert van t'Hoff, Gerrit Rietveld, and J. J. P. Oud, and nonobjective painter Piet Mondrian. Although van Doesburg's influence was especially noticeable in Paris and Germany, Mondrian's painting and Rietveld's furniture and architecture proved to be the most influential.

Rietveld translated Mondrian's basic, or "elemental," painting theories into buildings and furniture designs that stressed the relationship among lines, mass, and space. The architect allowed the function of an object or building to determine its form. This provided the basis for an application of Functionalism, which was to dominate avant-garde architecture and design for decades to come. Rietveld's *Red/Blue Chair* of 1917 exemplifies Modernist theory. Built from machined elements, the chair translated Mondrian's abstract, minimalist painting into a three-dimensional object.

GERRIT REITVELD:
END TABLE, ORIGINAL
DATE OF DESIGN, 1923
HEIGHT: 23 3/4"
TOP: 19 3/4" X 20 1/4"

The table, which was originally designed for the Schröder House, is constructed from only five elements, and painted in five colors. The colored surfaces of the table serve as visual compositional elements, almost negating their structural function. The weightless quality is further emphasized by the painted white edges, allowing the planes to float in space, thus "dematerializing" the volume. (From *Gerrit Rietveld: A Centenary Exhibition* October 3 - November 12, 1988, Barry Friedman Ltd., New York, p. 40.)

GERRIT RIETVELD:
**CHILD'S WHEELBAR-
ROW**, ORIGINAL DATE OF
DESIGN, 1923
13" X 28 1/4" X 11"

Having a large family,
Rietveld developed a
sensitivity to the needs
of growing children. In
1923, he designed
several toys, including
this brightly colored
wheelbarrow. (From
*Gerrit Rietveld: A
Centenary Exhibition*
October 3 - November
12, 1988, Barry Friedman
Ltd., New York, p. 42.)

GERRIT RIETVELD:

HANGING LIGHTING

FIXTURE, ORIGINAL DATE
OF DESIGN, 1920
HANGING SIZE: 53"
ADJUSTABLE BASE
PLATE: 15 3/4" X 15 3/4"
INCANDESCENT GLASS
BULBS AND OAK
BASEPLATE PAINTED BLACK

The simple composition
of three suspended
lighting elements was
an integral part of a De
Stijl environment. First
used in an interior
Rietveld designed for a
clinic in Maarssen, near
Utrecht, the original
installation featured an
additional, fourth tube
hung vertically, but the
design was later
modified when Rietveld
installed it in the
Schröder House in 1924.
Rietveld intended this
fixture to be compatible
with his furniture and to
harmonize with the
complex interior
coloration. (From *Gerrit
Rietveld: A Centenary
Exhibition*, October 3–
November 12, 1988,
Barry Friedman Ltd.,
New York, p. 37.)

RUSSIA

A s De Stijl was taking shape in the Netherlands, Russian Constructivism was developing a similar aesthetic, also based on the domination of the machine in design. With the events of the Russian Revolution of 1917, artists were able, for a brief period, to break radically with traditional art and architecture, and to experiment with abstract and geometric form. Their approach was even more radical than much of European Modernism. During the 1920s, the work of Russian artists and architects strongly influenced design in France, Germany, and the Netherlands.

Until the time of the revolution, Russia had been industrially backward. Its crafts tradition—local artisans creating objects for individuals—was somewhat akin to the approach advocated by Britain's Arts and Crafts theorists. After the revolution, Russian artists such as El Lissitzky, Konstantin Melnikov, Kasimir Malevich, and Vladimir Tatlin all designed a variety of projects for international exhibitions in the West that had a powerful impact on their contemporaries and helped to establish direct communication between the Constructivists and the De Stijl group as well as the Bauhaus.

El Lissitzky had studied engineering and architecture at Darmstadt, where one of his teachers was Olbrich, Peter Behrens's former partner. In 1920, El Lissitzky began teaching at the Vhkutemas in Moscow. This Soviet equivalent of the Bauhaus also employed Vladimir Tatlin, founder of Constructivism.

Tatlin believed that the role of the designer should not be as an artist but as an anonymous "worker" responsible for making the products for the new society. Although he is best known for his vast maquette for a monument to the "Third International Exhibition" of 1920, Tatlin also designed easy-to-wear workers' clothing.

Important work produced at the Vhkutemas included Modernist-inspired folding chairs of wood and metal designed by architect B. P. Zemlianitsyn and Modernist bentwood chairs designed by N. N. Rogozhin.

In 1921, Lissitzky, who by then had many international contacts, returned to Germany, where he met Moholy-Nagy, who was greatly influenced by the Russian's ideas.

However great the influence of Constructivist art and architecture was on Europe, the Soviet Union made its greatest contribution to Modernism through ceramics, many of which were designed by Malevich and Nikolai Suetin. According to historian Stephen Bayley, the works produced in porcelain from the Lomonossov factory were mechanical in feeling and abstract in decoration. Their designs are among the few totally successful integrations of ceramics and Modern art.

Suprematism, a form of abstract art pioneered by Malevich, was a major influence on Lissitzky and many European designers. Using minimal color—usually black and white—Malevich incorporated into his paintings abstract geometric motifs, which soon appeared on everything from fabrics to ceramics.

Although the abstract experiments of the Constructivists, Suprematists, and revolutionary Modern architects flourished in the Soviet Union during the 1920s, a great deal of the work remained only on paper. With Stalin's rise to power, Modernism was almost destroyed in Russia, as it was later in Hitler's Germany.

EL LISSITZKY:
CHAIR, 1930

This futuristic design
has been reissued by the
German manufacturing
company Tecta Mobel
for today's total design
consumers.

THE BAUHAUS AND
THE RISE OF MODERNISM

During World War I and immediately after, numerous styles continued to exist under the umbrella of what is now called Modernism. Not until the early 1920s and only after the Bauhaus had already been in existence did Modernism begin to focus on a single theme.

WALTER GROPIUS:
DESSAU BAUHAUS,
1925-1926

Belgian architect Henry van de Velde was a major influence on the early years of the Bauhaus. He designed the buildings where the Bauhaus was originally housed, and it was at his suggestion that Walter Gropius was offered the directorship. Much of the curriculum attempted to keep alive van de Velde's ideas.

When the Bauhaus officially opened in 1919 in Weimar, Gropius combined two existing schools, the Grand-Ducal Saxon Academy of Pictorial Art and the Grand-Ducal Saxon School of Arts and Crafts. Gropius's goal was to unite the fine and applied arts, giving them equal status. By creating this fusion, the Bauhaus was able to realize the goal of both the Arts and Crafts Movement and the Wiener Werkstätte.

The ideas behind the 1919 Programme of the Bauhaus reflected attitudes regarding art, architecture, and craft that had been shaped by developments in engineering and technology. During its brief existence, the Bauhaus precipitated a revolution in art education whose impact is still felt today. In the words of Wolf von Eckardt, "the Bauhaus created the patterns and set the standards of present-day industrial design; it helped to invent modern architecture; it altered the look for everything from chairs to book design. Among the various aims of the Bauhaus was to elevate the status of the crafts to that which the fine arts then enjoyed."

Under the directorship of Gropius, the Bauhaus successfully spread the tenets of Modern design and its relationship to industry—tenets originated by Peter Behrens in his work at AEG and in the charter of the Werkbund.

Many of the early teachers at the Bauhaus were Expressionist painters. The foundation course was taught by Johannes Itten, who instructed students in paper cutting and working with contrasts of light and shade. Gropius soon replaced Itten with Hungarian-born Constructivist Laszlo Moholy-Nagy, who

emphasized the role of structure and construction in the design processes and the use of geometric and abstract patterns.

Other teachers included painters Paul Klee and Wassily Kandinsky, who encouraged students to rediscover the basic properties of line and color and then to develop highly sophisticated ways of manipulating them.[11] Architect/ designers including Gerhard Marcks, Adolf Meyer, George Muche, Marcel Breuer, Josef and Anni Albers, and Herbert Bayer, and painters Lyonel Feininger and Oskar Schlemmer also taught at the Bauhaus over the years. In 1921–22, Theo van Doesburg first lectured at the Bauhaus on De Stijl ideas, consolidating the links between the two design forces.

In 1925, the Bauhaus moved to Dessau. The curriculum was changed to focus on ideas taken from the principles of interchangeability and standardization in mass production: that designing for industry meant the incorporation of basic units for the fabrication of products. The designs from the Dessau studios went directly to industry for mass production. Manufacturers began to produce housewares and furnishings, paying royalties to students, faculty members, and the school itself.

As C. Ray Smith has pointed out, this approach to design resulted in products styled to be efficient and functional. This simplicity of design came out of economic necessity. Shiny metal, richly veined stone, and nubby fabric were among the natural materials used to enrich the spare, functional designs. Structure based on rational design elements—along with clarity of parts and meticulous alignment—was the fundamental principle and the aesthetic effect of the new machine-based Modernism. It was a celebration of the machine, an aesthetic of machine-made production. The Bauhaus was the first group of designer/architects to acclaim Machine Age art.[12]

In 1926, five years after van Doesburg's first lecture at the Bauhaus, Mart Stam, an independent Dutch architect who had "invented" the first Modern tubular metal cantilevered chair, was invited by future Bauhaus director Ludwig Mies van der Rohe to contribute work to the 1927 Werkbund exhibition in Stuttgart. At about the same time, Mies van der Rohe and Marcel Breuer both designed tubular steel chairs using industrial processes.[13] At the Bauhaus, Breuer and van der Rohe mainly designed furniture. Breuer's wooden, tubular steel, and aluminum

MARCEL BREUER:
WASSILY CHAIR, 1925
TUBULAR STEEL, POLISHED
CHROME FINISH WITH
LEATHER SEATING
16 1/2" X 31" X 27 1/2"

Breuer's chair has won design awards at the Museum of Modern Art in New York and was recognized as a "Piece of Art" by the West German press when exhibited there in 1982.

furniture reflected the influence of De Stijl.

The statements of Mies van der Rohe that "less is more" and "God is in the details" illustrate his insistence on perfectionism in both his standards of design and the philosophy behind them.

Mies designed the German pavilion for the 1929 "International Exhibition" in Barcelona as well as the "throne chairs" of hand-buffed steel and leather. As Stephen Bayley points out, the pavilion was perhaps the perfect statement of the Bauhaus belief in total design: no detail was too peripheral or mundane for the attention of the designer. However, the pavilion also encapsulated much of the irony of Modernism. Despite the Modernists' acknowledged commitment to ideals akin to those of the Arts and Crafts Movement, Modernist products were not to the liking of much of the general public. Nor could the public afford to purchase them, because the materials were expensive.

American architect Frank Lloyd Wright was another influence on Mies van der Rohe, who wrote: "The work of this great master presented an architectural world of unexpected force, clarity of language, and richness of form. Here, finally, was a master builder drawing upon the veritable fountainhead of architecture, who with true originality lifted his creations into the light." Mies built very little before he left Europe to work in the United States. What he did construct evidenced a sleek, sophisticated Modernism that reflected a Germanic tradition of simplicity and lack of adornment.

LUDWIG MIES VAN
DER ROHE:
BRNO ARMCHAIR, 1930
TUBULAR STAINLESS STEEL
POLISHED FINISH,
CONSTRUCTED HARDWOOD
SEAT AND BACK FRAME
18" X 25 3/4" X 22 3/4"

This chair was designed
for the interior of the
Tugendhat House at Brno,
Czechoslovakia,
also designed by Mies.

LUDWIG MIES VAN
DER ROHE:
CHAISE LOUNGE, 1929
TUBULAR STAINLESS STEEL
POLISHED FINISH WITH
LEATHER UPHOLSTERY
25 1/2" X 70 1/4" X 31 3/4"

Mies van der Rohe's
classic chaise design
has won numerous
awards, including one
from the Museum of
Modern Art in New York
in 1977 and the Design
Center Stuttgart in West
Germany in 1978.

LUDWIG MIES VAN
DER ROHE:
THE GERMAN PAVILION,
1929

In 1929, Mies van der
Rohe designed the
German pavilion for the
International Exhibition
in Barcelona, Spain.
Considered by many to
be the "temple" of
Modernism, it reflected
the Bauhaus belief in
total design. It also
exemplified one of the
controversies that
surrounded much of
Modernism—its design
and furnishings were
made from expensive
materials, handcrafted,
causing products to be
too costly for the
average consumer.

FRENCH MODERNISTS

Another equally powerful representative of Modernism was French architect/designer Charles-Edouard Jeanneret, who changed his name to Le Corbusier. In 1925, Le Corbusier designed the Pavillon de l'Esprit Nouveau for the "Paris Exhibition," which inspired an entire generation of designers. Between 1928 and 1929 with his cousin, Charlotte Perriand, he designed a series of chairs, notably the chaise longue, which have become icons of Modernist design.

Even though Le Corbusier dominated the French architectural scene of the 1930s, other styles allowed Modernism to be seen through a diversity of objects and influences that caused the movement to strengthen its position throughout the world. Art Deco provided the luxury of decoration as did such styles as neo-Romantic and neo-Baroque—all of which appeared in various design formats at the 1925 "Paris Exhibition." Simultaneously the fine art styles of Cubism and Surrealism were reflected in clothing and the decorative arts.

Modernism and its variations were widely accepted in France. Noted French architects such as Robert Mallet-Stevens and Pierre Chareau experimented with their own forms of Modernism; Mallet-Stevens's furniture designs reflect the influences of Cubism.

Pierre Chareau designed a series of Functionalist furnishings using wood and iron. He also collaborated with Dutchman Bernard Bijvoet on the Maison de Verre in Paris, an architectural landmark that continues to influence architects today. The design, built between 1928 and 1932, called for the use of steel on the exterior structure. The interior incorporated specially designed furnishings and studded rubber flooring. Concerned with the total aesthetic of the structure, Chareau and Bijvoet designed the interior furnishings to reflect a sophisticated integration with the exterior shape.

LE CORBUSIER:
CHAISE LONGUE, 1927
HIGHLY POLISHED
CHROME-PLATED TUBING
WITH WEBBED SPRINGS,
UPHOLSTERED IN LEATHER
24 1/3" X 66"

Le Corbusier's chaise longue has become a classic of Modernist design from the 1920s.

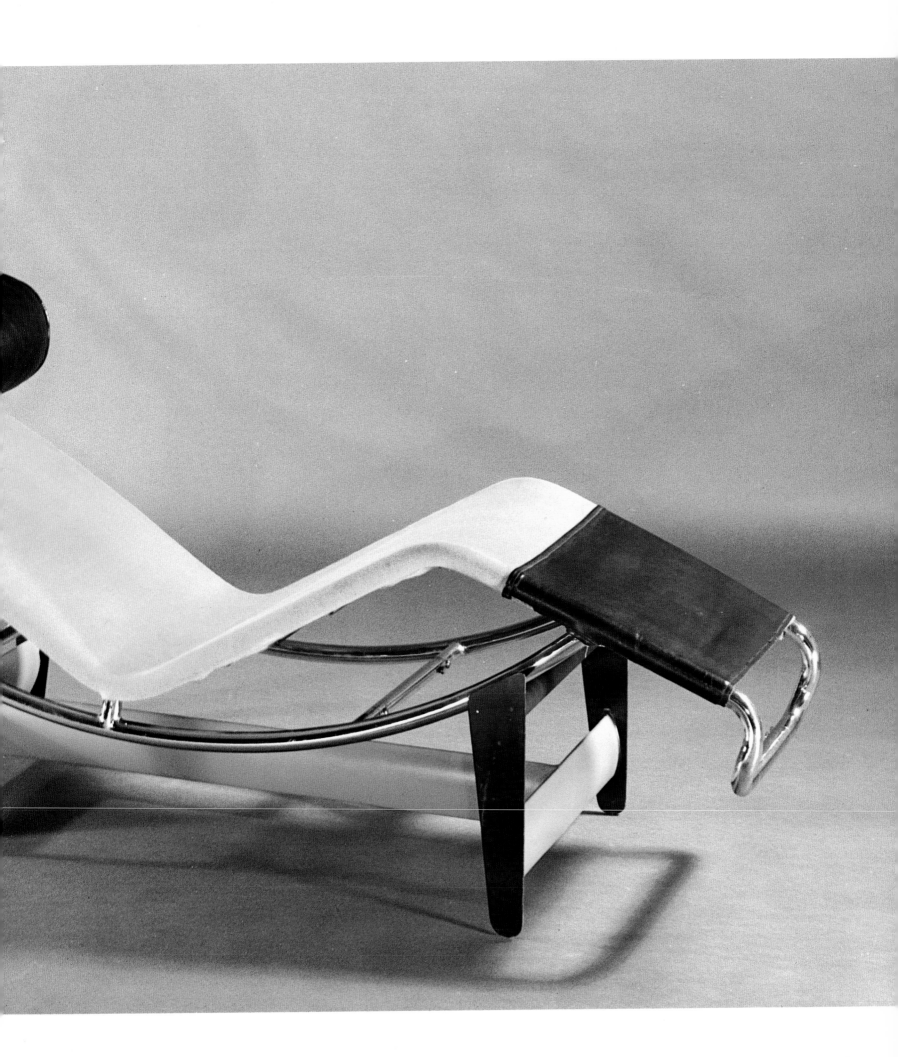

THE INFLUENCE OF ART DECO

[D] uring the 1920s, two major international design styles appeared simultaneously—the Classicism of Art Deco and the Modernism of the machine. Le Corbusier, along with several contemporaries in France, and the Bauhaus in Germany endorsed Modernism; Art Deco became one of the most popular styles in France and the United States.

In his book *Art Deco*, Bevis Hillier notes that Art Deco was an assertively modern style that drew inspiration from various sources including the more austere side of Art Nouveau, Cubism, Russian ballet, Native American art, and the Bauhaus. Unlike Art Nouveau, Art Deco emphasized geometry rather than asymmetry, and the rectilinear rather than the curvilinear. Proponents of Art Deco responded to the capabilities of the machine and of new materials such as plastics, ferroconcrete, and glass. Their ultimate aim was to end the old conflict between art and industry and the snobbish distinction between artist and artisan, partly by encouraging artists to become adept at their craft and by adapting designs to the requirements of mass production.

The 1925 "Exposition Internationale des Arts Decoratifs et Industriels Modernes" in Paris for many signified the introduction of Art Deco. Although machine designs were prominent in the exhibition, the innovative styles found in much of the French decorative arts dominated. Motifs were taken from ancient Egyptian, archaic Greek, and Mayan sources. Use of colors and patterns borrowed from earlier art movements such as Cubism, Fauvism, Futurism, and Expressionism.

Art Deco products incorporated exotic materials. Woods such as olive, burr walnut, Cuban mahogany, and ebony had inherently beautiful, natural colors. In combination with veneers and inlays of ivory and mother-of-pearl, these woods were used to create geometrically designed furnishings. Tortoiseshell, leather, snakeskin, and shagreen (green-dyed sharkskin) were employed as furniture upholstery, and lacquer was used extensively for many other decorative pieces.

In the period immediately following World War I, the emigration of many European architects and designers brought the tenets of European Modernism to the United States, where both Art Deco and international Modernism existed

MICHEL DUFET:
DESK, 1930
3'2" X 6' X 2'6"

Created in zinc as a reception desk for La Compagni Asturienne Des Mines (a zinc mining company) and also exhibited at the Salon Des Artistes Decorateurs. It was also in the Paris-Moscow exhibition at the Pompidou Center.

FRANK LLOYD WRIGHT:
DESK AND CHAIR,
C. 1936-1939
PAINTED STEEL AND
WALNUT

This office furniture
designed for use in the
Johnson buildings
reflects the curves and
circles found in the
building's architecture.
The chair is unusual in
gaining support from
only three legs. Wright
also designed the seats
and backs to be
reversible so they could
be flipped over to even
the wear.

simultaneously. The coexistence of the two styles can be seen in two of the most famous buildings in the United States: the 1929 Chrysler Building in New York by William Van Alen, a monument to the abstract, geometric motifs of Art Deco, and the 1936 house, Falling Water, in Bear Run, Pennsylvania, by Frank Lloyd Wright, a perfect example of international Modernist architecture.

During this period, other landmark Art Deco buildings were erected in New York City. Like the Chrysler Building, the Chanin Building, the Empire State Building, and Radio City Music Hall reflected the geometric lines of the period, their facades decorated with chevrons, sun motifs, and other Art Deco ornamentation.

FRANK LLOYD WRIGHT:
FALLING WATER,
1936
BEAR RUN, PENNSYLVANIA

Projecting from the rock base into which it is anchored, *Falling Water* almost grows out of the landscape. It is considered an embodiment of Wright's lifelong ideal of the domestic hearth, firmly rooted in natural surroundings.

THE 1930S

With the closure of the Bauhaus in 1933 and subsequent emigration of many of its members, the decorative arts and architecture in England and the United States became the beneficiaries of some of the "stars" from Europe. Breuer, Moholy-Nagy, and Gropius, as well as architects Berthold Lubetkin and Erik Mendelsohn, came to England. Breuer designed elegant Modernist furniture in plywood for the firm of Isokon from 1935 to 1937, then moved to the United States. His ideas for tubular steel furniture and the designs of various contemporaries, including Wells Coates and Serge Chermayeff, were put into large-scale production by the English firm, Practical Equipment Limited (PEL).

Gropius also left England for the United States and by the late 1930s was teaching with Breuer at Harvard University. Moholy-Nagy was appointed director of the New Bauhaus in Chicago in 1937, and the following year Mies van der Rohe left Germany for the United States. The New Bauhaus failed, and in 1939 Moholy-Nagy opened his own school, which by mid-1940s was called the Chicago Institute of Design. Continuing to use Bauhaus teaching methods, he placed a new emphasis on the use of "organic form" in design.

Another style of design, Neo-Classicism, which had been an important source of inspiration for Peter Behrens and Mies van der Rohe, was adopted by the architects of Nazi Germany and Stalinist Russia. Many apolitical architects who worked in the Neo-Classicist style instead of wholeheartedly embracing the doctrines of Modernism found their practices suffering, because Neo-Classicism became associated with Nazi Germany during the 1930s.

One of Britain's greatest architects, Sir Edwin Lutyens, exemplified the problem. Lutyens continued to design furniture, clocks, and light fittings in the Neo-Classicist style but with a sense of whimsy. Reflecting anti-Modernist themes, his work of the 1920s anticipated the metaphors and wit of Post-Modernism by half a century. But during this period his work came under harsh criticism, and his designs were considered out of step with the times.

The 1930s began with the trauma associated with the Wall Street Crash of 1929, followed ten years later with the outbreak of World War II. Designers with a more democratic philosophy, or with a shrewd eye for the market, made work appropriate to series production. These products included the traditional area of furniture and furnishings and the more novel categories of consumer items such as kitchen equipment and electrical goods, for which the 1930s saw a considerable increase in demand. A large and increasingly design-conscious middle-class market emerged despite the Depression.[14]

During the late 1920s in Scandinavia, the foundations were laid for an approach to Modernism that would become a major international influence after World War II. This style of design brought the Scandinavian respect for traditional crafts and preference for natural materials to the creation of new forms. According to Stephen Bayley in *Twentieth Century Style and Design*, before World War II, the Scandinavians had developed their own brand of Functionalism that was tempered by humanist concerns and was quite different in character from the attitudes of the Bauhaus. Responding to the need for objects and environments that were at once functional and inviting, Scandinavian manufacturers developed products that shunned exaggerated styling.

The leader in this new movement, Finnish designer and architect Alvar Aalto, designed simple yet practical furnishings in ply and laminated woods. His first designs from the early 1930s were created for the Paimio Sanatorium. The popularity of these designs inspired Aalto to establish his own manufacturing firm, Artek, in 1934.

In the years following World War I, experiments in architecture and design in Europe and the United States developed into a full-fledged progressive Modern architecture and design movement and influenced many of the efforts to revitalize the environment. The Modern movement embraced mechanization, standardization, and mass production while recognizing the need to incorporate aesthetics.[15]

Early Modernism flourished on the idea that humans could strive toward a state of harmony with their created environment and on the dream of a balanced relationship among man, machine, and product. Realizing these standards could improve design, educate the public, and bring commercial profit to manufacturers.[16]

ALVAR AALTO:

EASY CHAIR, 1936
SEAT AND BACK
UPHOLSTERED; SUPPORTING
CANTILEVERED SIDE PARTS
BENT AND LAMINATED

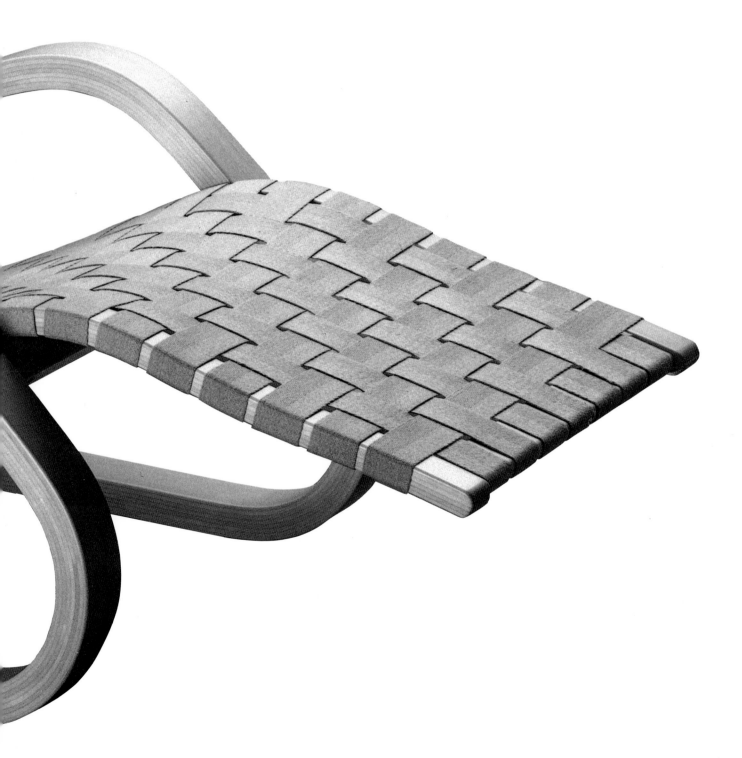

ALVAR AALTO:

CHAISE LOUNGE, 1937
LAMINATED FRAME
SUPPORTING CANTILEVERED
SIDE PARTS BENT AND
LAMINATED; WEBBED
COVERING

MODERNISM IN FRANCE

French Modernist furniture reflects a variety of influences and heritages—from angularity of cubism to the opulence of Art Deco—but it inevetibly shows a combination of imaginative design and technical proficiency.

PIERRE CHAREAU:
"T" STOOL, 1927
19" X 16" X 19 1/4"

The stool was created in 1927 and reproduced in mahogany for the Grand Hotel de Tours.

PIERRE CHAREAU:
THE NUN'S LAMP, C. 1928
WALNUT AND ALABASTER

This eccentrically designed lamp reflects Chareau's love of natural materials and the influences of Art Deco.

ROBERT MALLET-STEVENS:
CHAISE LONGUE, 1925
35 3/4" X 23 1/2" X 37 3/4"

Created for the garden of the villa of the Vicomte de Noailles in Hyères. The villa has since become the home of the Mallet-Stevens Foundation.

LE CORBUSIER:
EXTENDED LOUNGE CHAIR, 1928
HIGHLY POLISHED STAINLESS TUBING AND ANGLE STEEL FRAME WITH LEATHER UPHOLSTERY
24 1/3" X 39"

Le Corbusier's classic chair was intended as a series to compliment a two-seat sofa.

LE CORBUSIER:
LC/1 SLING CHAIR, 1928
HAND-FORMED STAINLESS STEEL TUBING. LEATHER SEAT.
25 1/2" X 25 1/6"

This classic sling chair of Modern design is included in the design collection of the Museum of Modern Art in New York.

MEDITERRANEE, C. 1927
HAND-KNOTTED WOOL
11'6" X 5'9"

This rug was used in the Roquebrune house.

ROBERT MALLET-STEVENS:
DINING CHAIR, 1930
32 1/2" X 14 1/2" X 16"

This dining chair was created for the cafeteria of the Salon Des Arts Menagers.

LE CORBUSIER:
LC/7 (SIEGE TOURNANT) ARMCHAIR, C. 1928

The Siege Tournant marks the appearance of support springs used as a base for a seat cushion; they radiate from the central point like spokes in a wheel, reiterating the theme of machinery, which was an important aspect of Le Corbusier's designs.

PIERRE CHAREAU:
FAN TABLE
2' X 2'

The two fan-shaped pieces are made of waxed, patinated wrought iron.

EILEEN GRAY:
TRANSAT ARMCHAIR,
1927
41 1/2" X 22" X 31"

This piece of furniture was also crafted for the Roquebrune house.

EILEEN GRAY:
SATELLITE MIRROR

This highly modernized mirror included a luminous porthole, an enlarging mirror, and a nickel-plated metal frame.

NEW BEGINNINGS

The years after World War II witnessed a remarkable outburst of creativity in crafts and decorative design and their application to mass production and industry. The United States, Scandinavia, Great Britain, and Italy became the new creative centers for this output. From these centers came a wide array of ideas and achievements, encompassing novel decorative styles, extraordinary craftwork, the refinement of traditional themes, styles inspired by the avant-garde in the fine arts, and a continual exploration of the Functionalist ideal.

In Great Britain, the government initiated a plan to raise the public's as well as manufacturers' standards and awareness of design. In contrast to the austerity of the war years, postwar design in Great Britain reflected the public's need for a more lighthearted style enlivened with humor and decorative indulgence.

By the mid-1940s, a number of countries, such as Britain, Germany, Finland, and Italy, realized that through innovative design they could reassert themselves within world trade. By bringing quality design to industry and emphasizing products made from the new materials, they would be more apt to realize economic recovery after the financial devastation of the war years.

The end of World War II was heralded in the United States by an economic boom. With this newly acquired prosperity came widespread building and consumerism. New materials and technologies, fostered by wartime research and development, were quickly assimilated into the marketplace. A wide range of synthetic materials helped to alter the world of design. The 1940s witnessed the birth of the age of plastics.

With the advent of a new middle-class market, designers had to adjust their ideas. Standards of taste were no longer set by an elite, to be sifted down to the lower classes. Nor did taste automatically reflect social standing, as it had in past decades. The demands of pervasive consumerism became a powerful force that had to be taken into consideration.

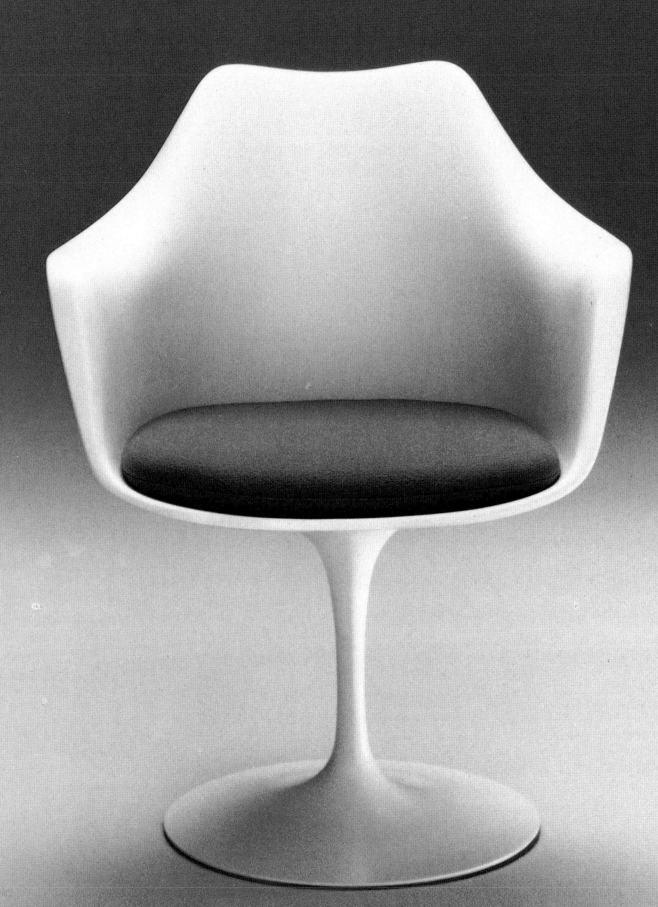

EERO SAARINEN:
TULIP ARMCHAIR, 1957

THE RISE OF FUNCTIONALISM

Functionalism, which gained prominence in the 1930s, became a key factor for design during the 1940s. The theory of Functionalism—that beauty in useful objects is defined by their utility and by honesty to materials and structure—was rooted in the mid-nineteenth century idea of "art in industry." This idea held that aesthetic judgments about objects could be made according to widely held standards, and that the exercise of these standards would improve design, educate the public, and bring commercial profit to manufacturers.[17]

The social goals of the International Style of the 1920s and 1930s failed to continue into the 1940s and 1950s. Its earlier aims focused on providing housing for the masses and on creating better work environments for everyone. By contrast, the International Style found in the United States at midcentury was manifested mainly in the construction of gigantic concrete and glass modules to house major corporations. The minimalism of Mies van der Rohe—the famous "less is more" doctrine of refining buildings to their fundamental elements—was adopted in the 1950s by big business. The pristine lines of the Miesian aesthetic formed the mainstream of the decade. The standard of the square module provided a unifying visual pattern that was repeated in high-rise apartment buildings and corporate headquarters throughout the country.

Modernism in the United States had been dominated by European architects, with the exception of Frank Lloyd Wright. In the 1940s, Wright studied the design of buildings as single geometric forms such as triangles and arcs. His subsequent projects consisted of repeated modular units such as triangles, hexagons, and circles. In the early 1950s, Wright built his first and only freestanding skyscraper, the H. C. Price Company Tower in Bartlesville, Oklahoma. Based on a 1929 proposal, the tower was both a residential and a studio complex with "double height and mezzanine spaces based on an interlocking plan of triangles and trapezoids and sheathed in copper panels, copper louvers, and glass." Wright designed furniture for these spaces that reflected his goal of consistent, integrated, total design. Made from cast aluminum forms, the furniture reiterated the elements of his architectural plans.

FRANK LLOYD WRIGHT:
TALIESIN, 1949
30 1/4" X 37" X 35 1/3"

This lounge chair was fabricated from flat plywood panels.

FRANK LLOYD WRIGHT:
H.C. PRICE COMPANY TOWER, 1953-1956
BARTLESVILLE, OKLAHOMA

The tower, similar in concept to an earlier Wright design, the Johnson Wax Administration Building in Racine, Wisconsin, was constructed of reinforced-concrete cantilevered systems covered in a glass membrane. The layout for the building as well as the furniture is based on a diamond-shaped module of 30- and 60-degree triangles; this design has also been scored on the floor throughout the building. The compactness of the plan and the angularity of the rooms and furnishings gives a sense of being on board a ship.

EERO SAARINEN:

WOMB CHAIR AND

OTTOMAN, 1946

16" X 20 1/2" X 40"

16" X 25 1/2" X 20".

Part of Saarinen's now-famous "organic modernism" design, the architect's *Womb Chair and Ottoman* have become classics, combining curvilinear natural forms with Functionalism.

THE CRANBROOK TRADITION

In 1926, due in part to the progressive vision and patronage of George C. Booth, Finnish architect/designer Eliel Saarinen built the Cranbrook Academy of Art in Bloomfield Hills, Michigan, which represented an updating of the Arts and Crafts tradition in a European-style design college. The teachers and students at Cranbrook were to make a contribution of international importance to the applied arts, notably in the 1940s and 1950s through the work of Charles Eames, Eero Saarinen, Harry Bertoia, and Florence Knoll.

The United States became a major force in furniture design during the 1940s and 1950s, and the nexus of much of this innovation was Cranbrook Academy under the direction of Eliel Saarinen. During the war years, American designers had a much greater degree of freedom of expression than did designers in Europe. The designers who studied and worked at Cranbrook Academy were especially influential on European design. Cranbrook also provided a spawning ground for a more decorative, yet abstract style of architecture that was highly original and American in its focus. Saarinen, who came out of the Arts and Crafts Movement and was a Modernist pioneer, provided a distinguished example of the open-minded designer possessing a wide range of skills.[18]

During the 1940s, three designers who came out of Cranbrook created innovative furniture and interior design. Eero Saarinen, the son of Cranbrook's founder, studied sculpture in Paris in the early 1930s before returning to Cranbrook in 1936 to teach with Charles Eames and Florence Schust. All three had trained as working architects, but only Saarinen continued to practice architecture on any large scale.

"GOOD DESIGN" AND
THE MUSEUM OF MODERN ART

[T]he Museum of Modern Art in New York played a major role in educating the public about good design. In 1940, Eliot Noyes, a recent graduate of Walter Gropius's program at Harvard, was appointed the first director of the museum's department of industrial design.

Both Noyes and Edgar Kaufmann, Jr., who succeeded him, promoted good design while arguing against unnecessary uses of styling such as the streamline designs of the late 1930s and early 1940s. Originating in shapes intended to move efficiently at high speed, the streamline style had been applied to a multitude of static objects. At MOMA, Noyes and Kaufmann exhibited only articles whose designs reflected their function.

This interpretation of useful design to mean "good design" was the basis for the promotion of Functionalism, which Noyes and Kaufmann accomplished through a series of "good design" furniture competitions organized first in 1940, then again in 1948. These competitions encouraged designers to create new furniture forms based on modern technology.

The first competition was "Organic Design in Home Furnishings." Noyes defined "organic" as the "harmonious organization of the parts within the whole, according to structure, material, and purpose. Within this definition there can be no vain ornamentation or superfluity, but the part of beauty is none the less great—in ideal choice of material, in visual refinement, and in the rational elegance of things intended for use." In the 1940 MOMA competition, Charles Eames and Eero Saarinen shared first prize for their jointly designed plywood chair. Eames and Saarinen brought about a revolution in furniture design. The decade's new materials and manufacturing techniques provided them with solutions to perennial problems not only in the design and construction of furniture but also in architecture.

Both designers evolved an organic, sculptural version of Modernism that seemed to fuse the curvilinear natural forms of Art Nouveau with the Functionalist philosophy of Modernism before the war. Their ideas and experiments, together and as individuals, extended beyond furniture to concepts of interior architecture.[19]

CHARLES EAMES AND EERO
SAARINEN:

MOLDED PLYWOOD CHAIR.

The original version of
this chair won Charles
Eames and Eero Saarinen
first place in the Museum
of Modern Art's "Organic
Design in Home
Furnishings" competition
in 1940. Charles and Ray
Eames revised the design
for mass production,
and Herman Miller began
distributing the chair
in 1946.

It combines wood and
metal in a technologically
and aesthetically honest
way that reveals
mechanical connections
instead of disguising
them. The rubber shock
mounts connecting the
bent chrome-plated steel
rods to the walnut veneer-
faced plywood are plainly
visible and as integral to
the design as the elegant
shapes of the seat, back,
and frame.

The molded plywood
chair has been called the
"most famous chair of the
century." *Time* magazine
nicknamed it the "potato
chip," and artist Saul
Steinberg once drew it for
The New Yorker with an
antimacassar draped over
its backrest, implying how
comfortable it is.

EERO SAARINEN:
GATEWAY ARCH,
ST. LOUIS, MISSOURI

In designing this monument, Saarinen said, "The major concern was to create a monument which would have lasting significance and should be a landmark of our time. An absolutely simple shape—such as the Egyptian pyramids or obelisks—seemed to be the basic of the great memorials that have kept their significance and dignity across time."

From 1936 to 1941, Eero Saarinen worked in his father's architecture office while collaborating with Charles Eames on the design of furniture. In 1946, Saarinen designed his famous, highly sculptural *Womb Chair*, and in 1948, he gained international recognition by winning the design competition for the Gateway Arch in St. Louis, Missouri. For architects of the following decade, Saarinen proved to be one of the most promising American practitioners.

Charles Eames, though trained as an architect, was best known for his furniture design. In 1941, he moved to California, where he first worked with molded plywood, initially producing leg splints for the U.S. Navy. It was this experimentation that led to Eames's design for the plywood-backed chair with splayed legs of chromed steel in 1945, followed by a curved plywood screen in 1946, and then by a fiberglass and steel chair in 1948. These designs shaped the organic style that became prevalent in furniture design during the 1950s. Eames's fiberglass chair won second prize in the 1948 "International Competition for Low-Cost Furniture" organized by the Museum of Modern Art in New York.

In the following year, 1949, the Museum of Modern Art began its series of "Good Design" exhibitions, which continued through 1955 and were major influences on furnishing design for years to come. Under Edgar Kaufmann's direction, the exhibitions played an important role in introducing the public to the aesthetics of good design. The 1949 show was designed by Charles and Ray Eames and traveled, as did future shows, to the Merchandise Mart in Chicago. Architects including Finn Juhl, Paul Rudolph, and Alexander Girard designed the "Good Design" exhibitions. Nearly every major American and European designer was represented in the five shows. The museum went so far as to build complete houses in its sculpture garden. For the 1949 show, Marcel Breuer designed his own interpretation of a Modernist home.

MANUFACTURING PIONEERS

T he creative climate of the 1940s encouraged links between designers and manufacturers. The results were innovative designs for mass production that established alternative ways for architects and designers to experiment with untried ideas.

Florence Schust, who worked briefly for Gropius and Breuer after she left Cranbrook, married Hans Knoll of the well-known German furniture firm in 1946. After Knoll immigrated to the United States in 1935, he established an equally successful design firm and employed Saarinen and Eames. Although the buildings designed by the Bauhaus immigrants had found a receptive audience in the United States, the appropriate furnishings had been unavailable.

In slightly more than a decade, Hans and Florence Knoll had established what became known as the "Knoll look" by commissioning significant Modernist furniture designs, many of which were to become icons for future designers.

Among the early products were Eero Saarinen's 1943 chairs of cut-out laminated wood frames with seats and backs of woven canvas strips. George Nakashima, another architect turned furniture designer, also produced pieces for the Knolls. Nakashima's highly individualistic furniture reflected early American styles as well as traditional Japanese forms and provided an innovative alternative to the machine-influenced furniture of the Modernists.

Knoll produced Saarinen's *Womb Chair* in 1948, making it the first known mass–produced, molded fiberglass-reinforced plastic shell. That same year, the company put Mies van der Rohe's *Barcelona Chairs* and *Stools* and his *Tugendhat Coffee Table* into mass production. Later the Knolls added the designs of Marcel Breuer to their line.

Florence Knoll designed for the firm seating units and wall-case pieces based on the modular concepts of De Stijl and Mondrian. Her designs championed mainstream Modernism and reflected the influence of Mies's minimalist elegance.

The ongoing research and development in new technologies provided designers with materials such as fiberglass, plywood, and steel, which lent themselves to organic, free-form treatment and innovative applications. Biomorphic motifs found both in the camouflage shapes of wartime materials and in the

CHARLES AND RAY EAMES:
LOUNGE AND OTTOMAN

Originally built in 1956 as a birthday present for Charles and Ray Eames's good friend, film director Billy Wilder, these were not intended to be mass produced. But thirty years later, Herman Miller had built more than one hundred thousand.

The chair is constructed of molded rosewood plywood with leather cushions and a polished aluminum swivel base. Brazilian rosewood veneer is selected, matched, and oil-finished by hand. Tufted leather cushions are hand-sewn to fit in the molded plywood forms. The base and back supports are attached with neoprene shock mounts that give the chair flexibility and resiliency. Winner of the Triennale Prize in Milan in 1957, the chair is in the permanent collection of the Museum of Modern Art in New York.

The designer is seated among the components of his "Action Office" system that he designed for Herman Miller in 1964.

work of such artists as Hans Arp, Joan Miró, and Alexander Calder began to appear in a wide variety of designs for furnishings in the 1940s.

Another manufacturer who supported the work of American designers was the Herman Miller Company of Zeeland, Michigan. In 1946, architect and author George Nelson began to design furniture for Herman Miller and soon became the firm's director of design. Multifaceted in his talents, Nelson also designed graphics, promotional materials, and showrooms, guiding the firm to a position as one of the two foremost producers of Modern furnishings in the United States. By the end of the 1940s, Herman Miller was producing Charles Eames's furniture designs and in the 1950s produced the work of architect/fabric designer Alexander Girard. In the 1960s, Herman Miller became the design laboratory for the American furniture industry.

While guiding Herman Miller, Nelson created some of the firm's most innovative designs, including the slat bench (1948), the headboard with adjustable backrest (1948), and the L-shaped desk (1949). For the next three decades, he designed numerous inventions for the furniture industry. Nelson demonstrated an extraordinary talent for conceiving entire environments. His freewheeling talent and unfettered vision enabled him to create innovative designs unhampered by past traditions. His concepts have made him one of the geniuses of twentieth century design, an accomplishment he attributes principally to clear thinking and hard work.[20]

With the introduction by the Herman Miller Company of Charles Eames's chair designs in 1946, Eames's goal of mass production and mass distribution was realized. The chair, a version of his earlier "potato-chip" chair, was produced in two heights—for dining and for lounging. Although it reflected the light, amorphic sculptural shape indicative of the period, it proved to have considerable structural strength and durability that belied the look of its design.

During the late 1940s, Eames continued to work with molded plywood and produced a number of pieces for Herman Miller, including a folding, molded plywood screen. In the 1950s, he designed a range of work that established him as the most innovative designer of the period and also influenced the

EERO SAARINEN:
TULIP ARMCHAIR, 1957
GLASS-REINFORCED
PLASTIC SEAT ON A CAST
ALUMINUM PEDESTAL
18" X 25 3/8" X 26"

Speaking of his tulip chairs, Saarinen said, ". . . as to the pedestal furniture, the undercarriage of chairs and tables in a typical interior makes an ugly, confusing, unrestful world. I wanted to clear up the slum of legs."

look of interiors throughout the United States. In 1950, he designed plastic shell chairs on spidery metal-rod legs, all-wire chairs in 1951, and plastic-shell stacking chairs in 1954. In 1958, he designed a large bent-plywood, leather-cushioned chair with premolded vinyl upholstery slings and matching leather-cushioned ottoman.

Although famous for his furniture, Eames designed and built one major architectural work, his own home in California. Like his other designs, the house also became an icon of design innovation. Built in 1949 in Pacific Palisades, it combined the machine imagery of Modernism with the found object aesthetic associated with Dada-Surrealism. The house was constructed from standard industrial metal and glass components ordered from manufacturers' catalogues, then assembled on site. It contained steel columns, open-web metal joists, and metal siding. Windows were constructed from transparent as well as translucent glass.

During this same period, the study of ergonomics became important to many designers, including Charles Eames. Pioneered by designer Henry Dreyfuss, ergonomics was concerned with the relationship of people to their environment. Eames applied Dreyfuss's findings to his mass-produced furniture designs for Herman Miller, developing forms that could be molded and stamped.

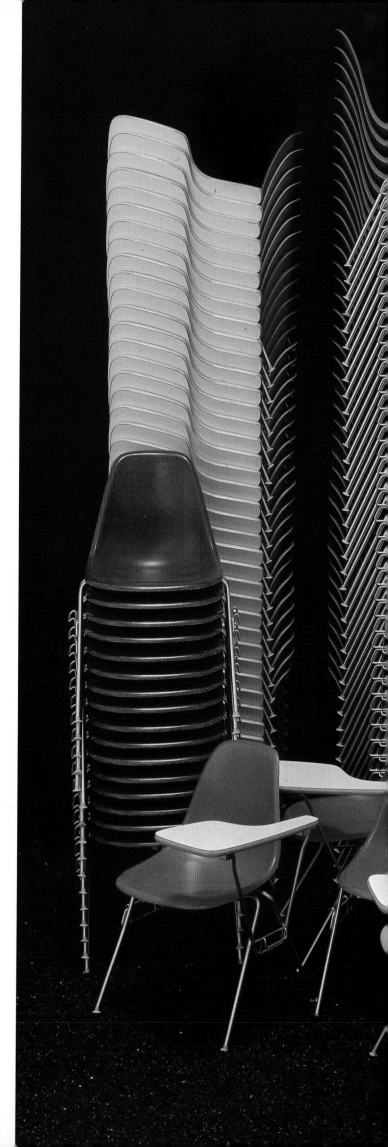

CHARLES AND RAY EAMES:
STACKING, GANGING, MOLDED FIBERGLASS CHAIRS

The boom in construction of civic and office buildings in the 1950s created a need for lightweight, durable chairs that could be easily used for additional seating. Among the first consumer products to use the materials developed by the aircraft industry during World War II, these molded shell chairs of fiberglass-reinforced polyester were prize-winners in the Museum of Modern Art's "Low-cost Furniture Competition" of 1948.

The armless version of this chair was introduced in 1952. This side shell chair won the First National Industrial Designers Institute Award Medal in 1951 and has been produced continuously by Herman Miller ever since.

An initial plan had been for the plastic pieces to be of metal, but by 1950 technology had advanced to the point where shaping plastic had many advantages over stamping out metal. The Eames plastic pieces are similar to earlier Eames forms and were manufactured with the ability to interchange the bases.

SCANDINAVIAN INFLUENCES

Scandinavian design, known in the 1930s as Swedish Modern, was recognized internationally as Scandinavian Modern in the 1940s. In the United States, the 1940s were known as the Scandinavian Decade. The designs, characterized by a blend of functionality with traditional styling, were seen as an interpretation of good taste and were found in middle-class households throughout Europe and the United States.

The designers, manufacturers, and craftsmen of postwar Scandinavia made products based on a philosophy similar to the ideals of the British Arts and Crafts Movement. Whereas the British designers chose to ignore the industrial revolution by following what became an unrealistic approach, designers in mid-twentieth century Scandinavian countries integrated design traditions and use of natural materials with modern technological innovations.

The work of the Finnish architect Alvar Aalto exemplified the reinterpretation of the Arts and Crafts style. Aalto was instrumental in formulating a national style that used local technology to make the most of natural resources, such as ply and other laminated woods, in simple, practical furniture forms.

Aalto's postwar work included major architectural projects in the United States and Scandinavia. Working within limitations caused by the lack of available raw materials, the severity of the Finnish climate, and a somewhat conservative, closely knit society, Aalto produced an individual style that reflected the order and discipline of Classicism.

Although the prevailing International Style of the period disapproved of any type of representationalism, Aalto continued to build and design in his personal style. He did, however, believe that architecture had the potential for instituting social change, a view expounded by such Modernist pioneers as Eliel Saarinen.

Danish Modernism was another style found within the Scandinavian design arena. Although quite similar to Scandinavian International Style, it had a softer elegance, based on handcraft rather than the machine.

ALVAR AALTO:
TEA TROLLEY, 1936-1937 LAMINATED BIRCH SIDE SUPPORTS, BENT INTO A CLOSED CURVE; TOP SURFACED WITH BLACK OR WHITE TILES AND A RATTAN BASKET

The tea trolley utilizes Finnish birchwood in a highly personal approach.

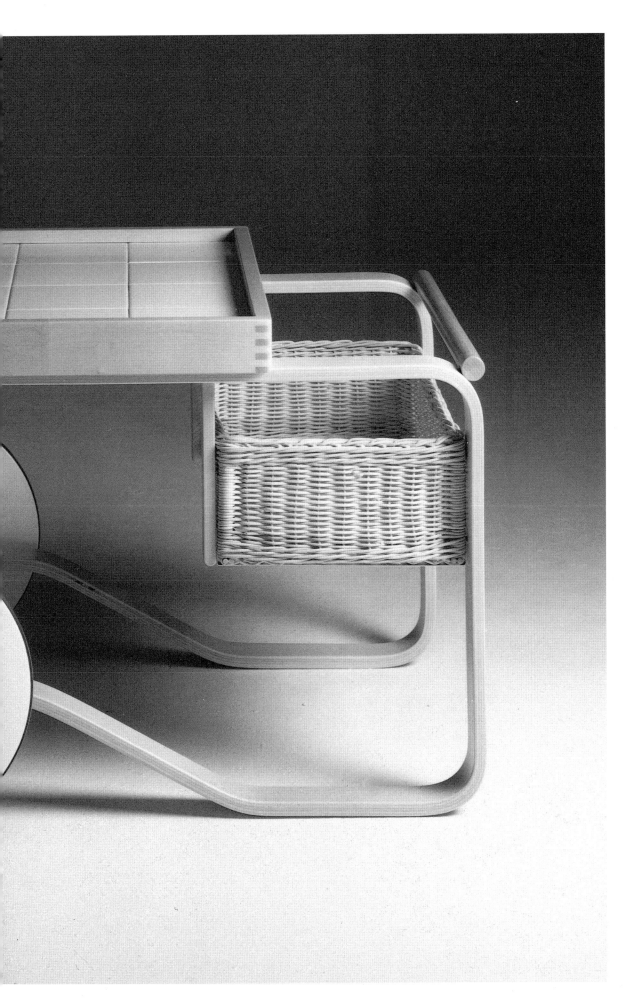

ALVAR AALTO:
EASY CHAIR, 1933
LAMINATED WOOD WITH
UPHOLSTERED SEAT AND
BACK

A classic of Modern
furniture design, using
bent laminated wood.

GUNNAR ASPLUND:

GOTEBORG,1, C. 1934-1937

31 1/2" X 15 2/3" X 20 1/2"

Gunnar Asplund, a
Swedish architect who
came to prominence as
the designer of the
highly influential
"Stockholm Exhibition"
of 1930, introduced
international modern
architecture to Sweden.
This chair reflects a
simplified Classicism
using natural wood
designs.

JOE COLOMBO:
STACKING CHAIR, 1965
NYLON AND
POLYPROPYLENE

Colombo's chair design
for the Italian firm
Kartell became an
instant icon. This was
the first all-plastic chair
to be made by injection
molding.

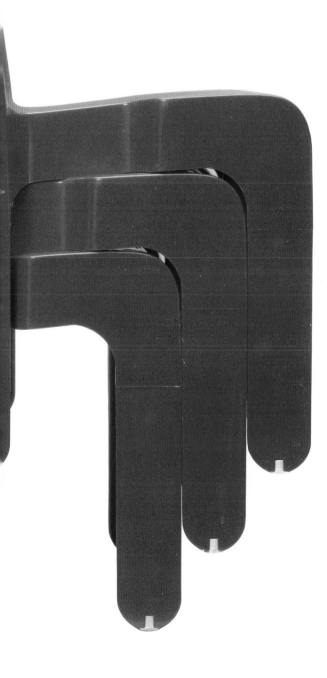

ITALIAN DESIGN

B y the end of the 1940s, Italian furnishings and interior design were becoming influential. The style was sculptural, reflecting humor and wit while possessing a clear, formal design logic. Italian designers quickly adapted American streamlining but created a more elegant version that they introduced into a wide range of products and furnishings.

The new generation of designers that emerged in the mid-1940s, such as Ettore Sottsass, Pier Giacomo Castiglioni, and Marco Zanuso, had been trained in the Rationalist tradition of 1930s architecture. Unemployed after the war, many went into interior and product design.

Experimenting with bent plywood, steel rod, glass, and eventually plastic, these designers were approached by several postwar furniture companies that previously had been craft workshops or were newly established to produce contemporary designs.[21] Companies such as Arteluce and Flos concentrated on lighting designs that were, in effect, functional pieces of sculpture. Technology and aesthetics developed hand in hand, resulting in countless innovative, highly expressive designs, all of which clearly reflected the post–Rationalist mood in Italian culture.[22]

Because of the commitment of a number of Italian manufacturing companies to quality design, mass-produced products reached a level of sophistication rarely equalled throughout the rest of the world. Companies such as Artemide, Cassina, Tecno, and Kartell employed such noted architect/designers as Joe Colombo, the Castiglioni brothers, and Marco Zanuso to produce innovative designs for everything from furnishings and housewares to plumbing fixtures. Several of the companies were run by designers whose farsighted visions encouraged ongoing research into the application of the newest technologies and materials.

Architect/designer Gio Ponti became a major figure through his wide-ranging and ever-inquisitive approach to design, through the inventiveness of his work in a wide variety of media, from architectural projects to decorative arts, and through his influence on the journal *Domus*. Ponti founded *Domus*, one of the first modern design magazines, in 1928. As one of the world's most influential design publications, it both increased the Italian design community's awareness of international achievements and promoted the work of the country's progressive designers.[23]

Ponti designed furniture for the Italian firm Cassina, including one of his most famous products, the "bulging" La Pavone coffee machine of 1949, and bathroom fixtures for the American firm Ideal Standard. In 1952, he designed what was to become a staple of inexpensive elegance—his personal version of the Chiavari-style chair.

The new Italian styles also reflected the furniture of Eero Saarinen and Charles Eames. The sculptural forms and organic curves of Italian designs illustrated a revamped Modernism. Italian designers used steel for the bases and frames of tables and chairs and for lighting fixtures.

Another major figure in Italian design was Turin architect/designer Carolo Mollino, whose work from the late 1940s combined logic and stylish invention. Using sculpted plywood, oak, or concrete, he created dramatically organic forms in architecture and furniture.

MARCO ZANUSO:

MAGGIOLINA, 1947
STAINLESS STEEL WITH
COWHIDE FILLED WITH
DOWN UPHOLSTERY
26" X 25 1/4" X 29 1/2"

Zanuso's lounge chair
won the gold medal in
the VII Triennale of
Milan. It is one of the
first projects with which
Zanuso presented a new
interpretation of the
rationalist tradition of
Italian design. This piece
is elegant in shape while
provide comfort.

A DECADE OF EXPANSION AND SYNTHESIS

During the 1950s, an explosion of juried exhibitions and awards for good design originated in the United States, then spread through Western Europe and Japan. Providing an important stimulus to progressive designers, the Museum of Modern Art's "Good Design" exhibitions under the direction of Edgar Kaufmann gave impetus to similar European exhibitions.

The main problem faced by Kaufmann in the selection process for the "Good Design" exhibits was the criteria requiring that the objects shown were actually available in the market-place. Kaufmann's "purism of functional design" was superseded by the realities of what was being mass–produced.

At the same time, Scandinavian design achieved wide-spread recognition through several international exhibitions including the Milan triennials of 1951 and 1954; a large exhibition of architecture, industrial design, home furnishings, and crafts at Hälsingborg, Sweden, in 1955, which was viewed by over one million visitors; and the "Design in Scandinavia" exhibition that toured North America from 1954 to 1957.

Although the objects included in the "Good Design" exhibitions at MOMA and the triennials in Milan ranged widely in style—from simple 1930s Functionalist designs to decorative handcrafts, to technological displays of laminates, alloys, and micromechanics—they were considered exemplars of a single Modernist aesthetic, defined by utility, efficiency, fitness of purpose, truth to materials, and economy of means. These shows were also distinguished by the single-minded vision of their respective jurors.[24]

A characteristic that emerged from the "Good Design" exhibitions, as well as from MOMA's low-cost furniture competitions, was designers' predilection for clean, unornamented shapes that could be mass-produced cheaply and which lent themselves to multiple uses. These simple styles, similar to the streamlined designs of the 1930s, could be repeated using new plastic materials and bonding techniques.

By the mid-1950s, the sensuous colors found in the color–field school of Abstract Expressionism found their way into Modernist designs. These colors were far more exciting than the primary colors that had been the staple of De Stijl-Bauhaus ideology.

Influenced by the color-field school, architect/designer Alexander Girard became a color consultant to the G. M. Research Center and in 1951 began to design fabrics for Herman Miller. Girard's fabrics contributed to the color revolution started by Abstract Expressionism, but also echoed the two-dimensional fabric patterns designed at the end of the nineteenth century by C. F. A. Voysey. Girard described his designs as incorporating "simple geometric patterns and brilliant primary color ranges." This approach was fundamental in his work through the 1970s. Girard also designed spectacular exhibition spaces, including two "Good Design" shows for the Museum of Modern Art. One of his inventive designs for an exhibition space used marqueelike light bulbs to define the interiors.

Because the International Style of the 1950s discouraged ornamentation of any kind in both decorative arts and architecture, patterned screens came into vogue. These devices provided texture and ornament while being functional objects that controlled lighting and privacy. Eames, Saarinen, Alto, and even Frank Lloyd Wright created screens. For the 1952 "Good Design" show, architect Paul Rudolph designed an innovative curve-plan screen made of folded cardboard between wood strips. California architects Campbell and Wong installed cut-and-pierced lattice Japanese screens for several interior exhibits.

By the mid-1950s, synthetic fibers and permanent forming or molding opened a new world of man-made materials: plastic sheeting and panels, vinyl upholsteries and drapery fabrics, artificial leathers and other coated textiles, and synthetic carpets. Plastics were used extensively for chair frames, tables, and other furniture and for every conceivable household appliance, utensil, and toy.

For those designers raised on the philosophy of honesty of materials, the 1950s was a painful time. Known as the Plastic Decade, it was a period of exuberance to the point of silliness. It was an age that favored cuteness in objects and design, objects that often were considered kitsch. Disneyland opened in California in 1955, and the flamboyant hotel designs in Miami

PHOTOGRAPH OF ALEXANDER GIRARD

Fabric design was only one aspect of Alexander Girard's expression. His architectural commissions often provided the impetus for a bold departure in fabric design. Girard's interiors were perfectly orchestrated demonstrations of how to use his fabrics effectively.

Beach and Las Vegas became the antithesis of the severity of international Modernism. The attitudes of the decade's vanguard provided a rebuttal to the age of kitsch.[25]

During the 1950s, the Modernists saw their International Style skyscrapers constructed throughout the United States, South America, and Europe. In 1951, Mies van der Rohe built the 860 Lake Shore Drive Apartments in Chicago, using a structural frame sheathed with a glass curtain wall. The lobbies were furnished with his Barcelona furniture from the late 1920s.

The rapid economic recovery of Germany after the war was due to the guidance of Konrad Adenauer and to the character of the German people, who showed fierce determination to rebuild their country. The rigorous approach to German design in the 1950s, which benefited from the strong foundation of applied design established before the war, was epitomized by the establishment of the College of Design, the Hoschschule für Gestaltung, in Ulm, West Germany in 1955. Inge and Grete Scholl, the school's founders, chose Swiss architect and minimal sculptor Max Bill as the first director and the designer of the school buildings.

Considered to be the most important school of design of the decade, the College of Design was a bastion of Functionalism. Max Bill envisioned it as a successor to the Bauhaus and sought to unify art and industry by training designers in the elements of form and mechanics. The school at Ulm was actually more successful than the Bauhaus. Although both programs took on commissions for industrial prototypes suitable for mass production, the College of Design had much stronger links with industry due to its more producible line of designs. One of the school's first projects was to design a series of combined radio and phonograph sets, and their displays, for Braun. Bill believed in the value of individual creativity and an artistic, intuitive approach to design with the aim of humanizing the products of modern industry. This Werkbund Arts and Crafts philosophy and the school's curriculum changed radically when he left the school in 1957.

An emphasis on "science and technology" replaced the fine arts at Ulm. The products showed a more conscious regard for the consumer. The study of ergonomics was introduced into the curriculum. Even though the applications of ergonomics

INSTALLATION BY ALEXANDER GIRARD

PHOTOGRAPH BY CHARLES EAMES

The interior of the Herman Miller Showroom in San Francisco, designed by Alexander Girard in 1958.

were few and far between during the 1950s, this innovative science came to have broad, international appeal in the decades to follow.

The International Style of the 1950s was as far-reaching as the Modernism from which it evolved. Some of the greatest Functionalist architects of previous decades dramatically changed the focus of their designs. Le Corbusier's interest in Functionalist ideas influenced the upswept curves and plasticity of the 1950s organic styles. His famous church of Notre-Dame du Haut at Ronchamp, begun in 1950 and completed in 1955, used concrete, but its curvilinear design had none of the sparsity of his earlier work. Walter Gropius was commissioned by the innovative German firm of Rosenthal to design a tea service. The result was "bulging in form but sculptural and streamlined," thus marrying two of the more prevalent styles of the 1950s.

Frank Lloyd Wright abandoned his rigid geometric forms in the early 1940s when he began the spiral concrete design for the Solomon R. Guggenheim Museum in New York, which was finally completed in 1959. Eero Saarinen also incorporated curves in his architecture, such as the shell-concrete roof for the Auditorium Building at Massachusetts Institute of Technology, completed in 1952.

By the end of the 1950s, the term *design* had gained international acceptance. It was synonymous with good taste, consumer appeal, and high exports on the world market. Trends in design development had become truly international. According to Penny Sparke, such events as the triennials in Milan and various other international design conferences and exhibitions encouraged the development of what has been called "the transatlantic mainstream modern look," a style based upon a neo-Bauhaus attitude but influenced by many national variants.[26]

FRANK LLOYD WRIGHT:
THE SOLOMON R. GUGGENHEIM MUSEUM, 1956-1959
NEW YORK CITY

Although the Museum is considered by critics and admirers alike to be an outstanding example of the expressive possibilities of reinforced-concrete construction, the interior's spiralling circular ramp inhibits the exhibition and viewing of the works of art.

THE AGE OF PLURALISM

By the end of the 1950s, the influence of Modernism was diminishing. With the continued expansion of consumerism, people no longer listened to the dictates of a design elite. While the Museum of Modern Art in New York was endorsing and exhibiting "good design" products, an alternative idea of American culture emerged. The impact of Hollywood movies, advertisements, and pop music quickly invaded the homes and streets of industrialized nations all over the world.[27]

Increased consumer wealth enabled a variety of styles to develop simultaneously. These radically altered concepts of design, encouraging the development of pluralism and eclecticism. Because the marketplace consisted of different subgroups—each with its own social, economic, and cultural context—design could no longer be narrowly defined. The pluralism of the market fed design variation, and Modernism, utterly inadequate in this situation, gave way to design alternatives.[28]

In the early 1960s, Functionalist rules began to yield to a more open-ended approach toward design and style. Built-in obsolescence and throw-away products that fulfilled short-term rather than long-terms needs became the norm in manufacturing. Manufacturers raced to keep pace with the demands for stylistic novelty in products. New looks were created from such previous styles as Victoriana, Art Nouveau, and Art Deco. The age of pluralism made Modernism seem stale, outworn, and unacceptable by a more individualist generation.[29]

RICHARD MEIER:
CHAIR, 1982

POP ART AND THE BEGINNINGS OF POST-MODERNISM

During the late 1950s and early 1960s, Pop Art emerged as a major force in the fine arts and also in all areas of design. Bright colors and synthetic, disposable materials were used in ways not thought of previously. Furniture was designed in primary-colored plastics and printed cardboards. The imagery in the sculpture of Claes Oldenburg and the painting of Andy Warhol was reflected in everyday products from domestic linens to furniture.

Pop Art incorporated everyday objects that symbolized throw-away popular culture. From advertising, roadside billboards, and commercial imagery to household items, comic strips, television, and movies, these emblems of mass culture were quickly integrated into the vernacular of architecture and design. By the mid-1960s, the extreme Minimalism found in the International Style had been openly challenged by Pop. The colors and designs found in psychedelic art, another aspect of Pop culture, appeared in all areas of design. The whiplash curve of Art Nouveau was rediscovered and updated with phosphorescent Day-Glo colors.

The development of Post-Modernist design in the 1960s is related to the development of Pop Art; both represented a reaction against the ideas of "good form" originally espoused by the architects of the 1930s and carried through the 1950s. Post-Modern architects and designers have created a vernacular that relies on recognizable historical points of reference. Their approach emphasizes exaggerated ornamentation, innovative materials, humorous patterns, and a broad spectrum of colors.

In 1961, a "think tank" of young English architects who used the Pop style in their designs formed the group Archigram. This was followed a few years later by the formation of Archizoom and then Alchymia, both in Italy. Archizoom was led by architect/designer Andrea Branzi, who later worked for Alchymia and then for Memphis.

Working at Archizoom, Branzi and Paolo Deganello were concerned with creating a revolutionary approach to design applications. Archizoom produced *Dream* beds in 1967 and *Mies* chairs in 1969. Their work satirized the "good design" prerequisites of the Museum of Modern Art exhibitions of the 1940s and the Milan trienniales of the 1950s.

PAOLO DEGANELLO AND GILBERTO CORRETTI: **ARCHIZOOM SEATING SYSTEM**, 1975, 1978, 1979

The Archizoom Seating System reflects both Modernist sleekness and a Pop idiosyncrasy, a combination typical of Post-Modern design.

LUDWIG MIES VAN
DER ROHE IN ASSOCIATION
WITH PHILIP JOHNSON:
SEAGRAM BUILDING,
1959
NEW YORK CITY

Reflecting the "less is
more" philosophy to its
fullest interpretation, the
towers appear to have
been reduced to almost
nothing in terms of
decorative effect.

MODERNISM
REFINED AND REEVALUATED

W hile Pop Art encouraged a design counterculture based on the disposable and the superficial, the persistence of a revamped Modernism stressed the pre–World War II rectilinear style of pure lines and forms and uncluttered surfaces. Viewed by many as "curtain-wall Minimalism," the Modernism of the 1960s quickly came under attack as the youth of the decade rebelled against the materialism of the period.

Two fine art movements of the 1960s, Op Art, or optical illusion art, which incorporated hard-edged abstract patterns, and Minimalism, which used three-dimensional structures of simplified form and flat color, appropriated the strong, geometric elements of early Modernism. The hallmarks of these movements were quickly taken up by many architect/designers who continued to work in the Modernist vein.

Whereas Bauhaus and other designers of the 1930s had only simplified ornamentation, Modernist designers of the 1960s refined the "less is more" principle to its ultimate. This postwar generation of architect/designers eliminated ornamentation. The resulting creations were seen by many as just white plaster boxes with bare floors, ceilings, and walls. Door and window openings eschewed trim, the openings remaining flush with the wall. These minimalists of the 1960s took Bauhaus goals to their apogee of refinement.

Completed in 1959, the Seagram Building in New York City, by Mies van der Rohe in collaboration with Philip Johnson, embodied Mies's idiom of total design. Many other buildings and interiors were developed with the same goal of total design: the Four Seasons Restaurant in New York City, also designed by Philip Johnson, in 1959; Alexander Girard's La Fonda del Sol, a restaurant in New York's Rockefeller Center complex, in 1960; and Eero Saarinen's sculptural TWA Terminal at JFK International Airport, in 1962.

Saarinen's design for TWA included sculptural furniture that seemed to grow organically out of the floor. Throughout the building, in fact, no distinction was made between the architecture, interior design, and decoration. Like Saarinen's design for TWA, many showrooms, retail stores, and restaurants reflected the Miesian principles of coordinating a building's exterior and interior with furnishings and other appointments.

During the 1960s, the design firm of Knoll Associates helped to promote Modernism by opening showrooms on an international scale. Changing its name to Knoll International, the company quickly became one of the world's largest design service and manufacturing retailers for Modern furniture. By the mid-1960s the "good design" of Modernism was being marketed at reasonable prices to the general public through such stores as Design Research, Marimekko of Finland, Azuma, and the Pottery Barn.

In 1963, architect/designer Paul Rudolph built the Art and Architecture Building at Yale University in New Haven, Connecticut. It opened to a controversy that to many began to signal the end of Modernism's viability. Rudolph's totally designed structure had special furniture and wall treatments of ornamented details and friezes. Although the building prophesied the role of art in architecture for the next decade and the role of art history in architecture for the next two decades, the building represented a major contrast between two very diverse viewpoints in design.

Many Modernist architects and designers considered Rudolph's structure the most innovatively designed building since Frank Lloyd Wright's Larkin Building or Mies van der Rohe's Tugendhat House. It completely integrated all architectural elements, including mechanical systems, work spaces, finishings, and furnishings.

But those who had to use the building—the faculty and students—thought it was a failure. The studio facilities and work spaces were poorly thought out; much-needed ventilation for certain areas was nonexistent; and access to and from basement sculpture studios was so undersized that large-scale projects were unable to be built there. The structure actually dictated the type and size of work that could be created within its confines.

During this controversy, the Modern movement began to be questioned. Rudolph's building was not the only structure with problems. According to historian C. Ray Smith in his book *Interior Design in 20th–Century America: A History,* integration of

structural and mechanical systems, the consistent design of exterior and interior, and the multiple and overlapping functions of these and other elements were often achieved at the expense of efficient use and customary activity. Too often, form only followed design function, not user function or activity function, and rarely psychological function. Innovation was more important to some Modernist designers than the cultural habits, traditions, and expectations of users or occupants of the interiors and buildings.

Although an increasingly wider gap appeared in the 1960s between the promises and the reality of Modernist applications, the majority of architects working during the 1960s continued in the Modernist vein even as a third generation of Modernists, including Robert Venturi, Charles Moore, Philip Johnson, and Paul Rudolph, gained prominence.

Practitioners of the International Style were accused of replicating Miesian copies of Chicago and Manhattan throughout the United States and Western Europe. It was becoming apparent that the utopian cities Modernist architects had promised would replace slums had not been built, and those projects that had did not live up to their supposed functions. Nor had the goals of creating better ways of living and working for the public been realized. Many of these Modernist buildings were technically flawed and unrealistically planned.

PAUL RUDOLPH:
**YALE ARTS AND
ARCHITECTURE
BUILDING**, 1963
NEW HAVEN,
CONNECTICUT

Rudolph's complicated and controversial building exemplified the architect's approach of separating the building's functions from one another to make their purpose visible from the outside.

THE 1970S

The Art Nouveau curvilinear style from the 1920s and 1930s, revived by the Pop culture of the 1960s, became a pivotal motif during the 1970s. Historicism, Classicism, and decoration, which made up the platforms of the vanguard architect/designers of the 1960s, were quickly assimilated into the mainstream by the 1970s.

Early in the decade, Functionalism was discredited by a variety of events in architecture and design. The traditional belief in aesthetic value, which had made Functionalism a universal design standard, came under attack from various segments within the design community. The influential writer/ architect Charles Jencks wrote in his book *The Language of Post-Modern Architecture*: "Happily we can date the death of Modern architecture to a precise moment in time. Modern architecture died in St. Louis, Missouri, on July 15, 1977." Jencks was describing the date that the Pruitt-Igoe high-rise blocks, built only twenty years earlier, were demolished due to structural problems and other failings.

Studies done during the 1960s and 1970s on users' needs in the home and workplace resulted in a greater awareness of interior architecture. Designing for the needs of people—an idea espoused by the members of the Bauhaus and by designers in subsequent decades—was put into actual practice. Many manufacturers in the mid-1970s were forced to deal with product safety, durability, conservation, ecology, ergonomics—all of which came under the umbrella of humanistic design. Many designers began to specialize in these areas, and as a result many design firms, especially in the United States where safety regulations were strict, played an important part in these fields.

The 1970s also saw a revival of interest in natural materials and the traditions associated with the work of craftsmen. The oil crisis in 1973 caused many architects to alter their design focus since many Modernist elements, such as glass-curtain walls, were not energy efficient.

While designers in general were assimilating Modernism into a simplified, refined version of Minimalism, another group of architect/designers began to rebel against established Modernist aesthetics and to use decoration, ornamentation, and historical references in their designs.

WARREN PLATNER:
THE PLATNER COLLECTION, 1973

Platner's design for this collection of office furnishings are sleek and elegant yet remain sturdy and functional.

VENTURI, RAUCH AND
SCOTT BROWN:
**TREE HOUSE, NEW
CHILDREN'S ZOO**, 1985
PHILADELPHIA ZOOLOGICAL
GARDENS

When Venturi, Rauch
and Scott Brown was
commissioned to design
the new Children's Zoo,
part of the program
called for the creation of
a special exhibit area to
aid visitor understanding
and sympathy with the
natural world and the
conceptual world of
science. Thus the most
important element in the
zoo became the reuse of
an architecturally
distinguished Victorian
building to house a
series of innovative,
interactive exhibits
depicting different
animal and plant
environments.

THIRD-GENERATION MODERNISTS

The spokesmen and leaders of the third-generation Modernists were architects Robert Venturi, Charles Moore, Philip Johnson, and Paul Rudolph. These designers and their followers rebelled against the rigid formality of the past and the regimentation of many established designers. They were more interested in furniture systems that involved users' needs and were adaptable to the psychological as well as the physical requirements of an environment.

Rejecting pure, clean, geometrically styled structures and furnishings, this new generation espoused Modernism's opposites: historicism and ornamentation. Design was once again varied. Color, pattern, and ornament—historical traditions rejected during the tight reign of International Style—were incorporated into all areas of design.

It was Robert Venturi and Charles Moore, especially, who reintroduced historical allusions into the design world. At first they resisted the term Post-Modernism, popularized by Charles Jencks, to describe their innovative philosophies and styles.

Venturi, one of the most influential critics of the Modern movement, published *Complexity and Contradiction in Architecture* in 1966. Even though Venturi always considered himself part of the Modern movement, his views have had a crucial role in the birth of Post-Modernism. Although he is a product of Modernism—having worked for both Eero Saarinen and Louis Kahn before establishing his own practice with Denise Scott Brown and John Rauch—Venturi attacked the Functionalism and reductionist aesthetics of Mies van der Rohe.

Modifying Mies's infamous "less is more" to "less is a bore," Venturi believed that he could take into account the activity patterns of his clients while maintaining historical continuity in his designs. As historian C. Ray Smith has noted, this recognition and acceptance of the contradictions in architecture led Venturi to a new and complex view of how design professionals could be more in step with the needs of users.[30]

In his second book, *Learning From Las Vegas*, Venturi promoted the need for architecture "to grow from popular culture as well as from high art to incorporate the symbolic values with which users like to invest buildings and to absorb the unconscious vernacular of those buildings that have never seen an architect."

Charles Moore, another Post-Modernist who studied with radical Modernist architect Louis Kahn before starting his own practice in 1965, also emphasized the use of decoration in design and is known for the humor and informality of his architecture. Moore believed that architecture is "territoriality" and "that it is the architect's responsibility to create a sense of place in space, time and the order of things." He has also stated: "We do not reject games, postures or the apparently arbitrary fancies and associations of those for whom we build, but rather seek to fashion from these a sensible order that will extend our own and our users' ability to perceive and assimilate the delights and complexities of an untheoretical world."

Moore's work reflects inspiration from a wide variety of sources, including high style and vernacular examples from the history of architecture, as well as the principles and forms associated with Louis Kahn. This has often led Moore to create designs or decorations that are sometimes picturesque or Pop in quality and which jar the eye while stimulating the mind. [31] In 1975, Moore designed a new urban square in New Orleans that incorporated a fountain symbolizing in three dimensions a map of Italy and including cutouts and neon.

With Philip Johnson's design in 1978 for the AT&T headquarters in New York, historicism gained acceptance in the commercial marketplace. Johnson's design, which has been compared with a Chippendale tallboy, is divided into three elements reflective of Art Deco skyscrapers. It is made up of a base that is loosely modeled on Brunelleschi's Pazzi chapel, a shaft that rises up the main facade of the building, and a broken-pediment top.

By the mid-1970s, the Post-Modernist architects, in their rebellion against the International Style, had adopted ornamentation that was flattened, outlined, and silhouetted. Some of the designs contained simplified three-dimensional Classical motifs, brightly painted in multiple colors.

The term *Post-Modernism* was adopted by a small segment of the architecture and design community to explain their work. For them it meant borrowing, manipulating, and applying historical traditions, especially Classical architecture and decoration. The Post-Modernists revived interest in the styles of such architects as Sir Edwin Lutyens, Alvar Aalto, Paul Cret, and Josef Hoffmann. They also adapted the styles of the Georgian periods, the lattices and grids of the Wiener Werkstätte, and the shingle style. Period ornamentation and forms were assimilated into a system of Classical ornamentation for present-day use.

As C. Ray Smith explains in *Interior Design in 20th–Century America: A History*, the straightforward expression of all building elements, which had been the goal of the Functionalists since the 1920s, was again popularized in the 1970s. Only now it was taken to extremes. This can be seen in the design of the Centre Georges Pompidou in Paris, completed in 1978. The ultimate expression of Functionalism and "high–tech" design, the building has its structural and mechanical systems on the exterior as a kind of superscale, Tinker-Toy decoration.

The designers of the 1970s who continued to follow the tenets of Modernism took industrial and industrial-looking materials out of their usual context and used them for every aspect of interior architecture including furnishings. This approach took a seventy-year-old attitude toward mass production and popularized it for the widest-possible audience.

Since the 1950s, Modernism has continued to be a force in design, but its utopian promises have been replaced by a more intellectual view of Functionalism. This high–tech or industrial style incorporates such products as metal shelving, studded rubber flooring, laboratory glassware, and medical trolleys into everyday living and working environments.

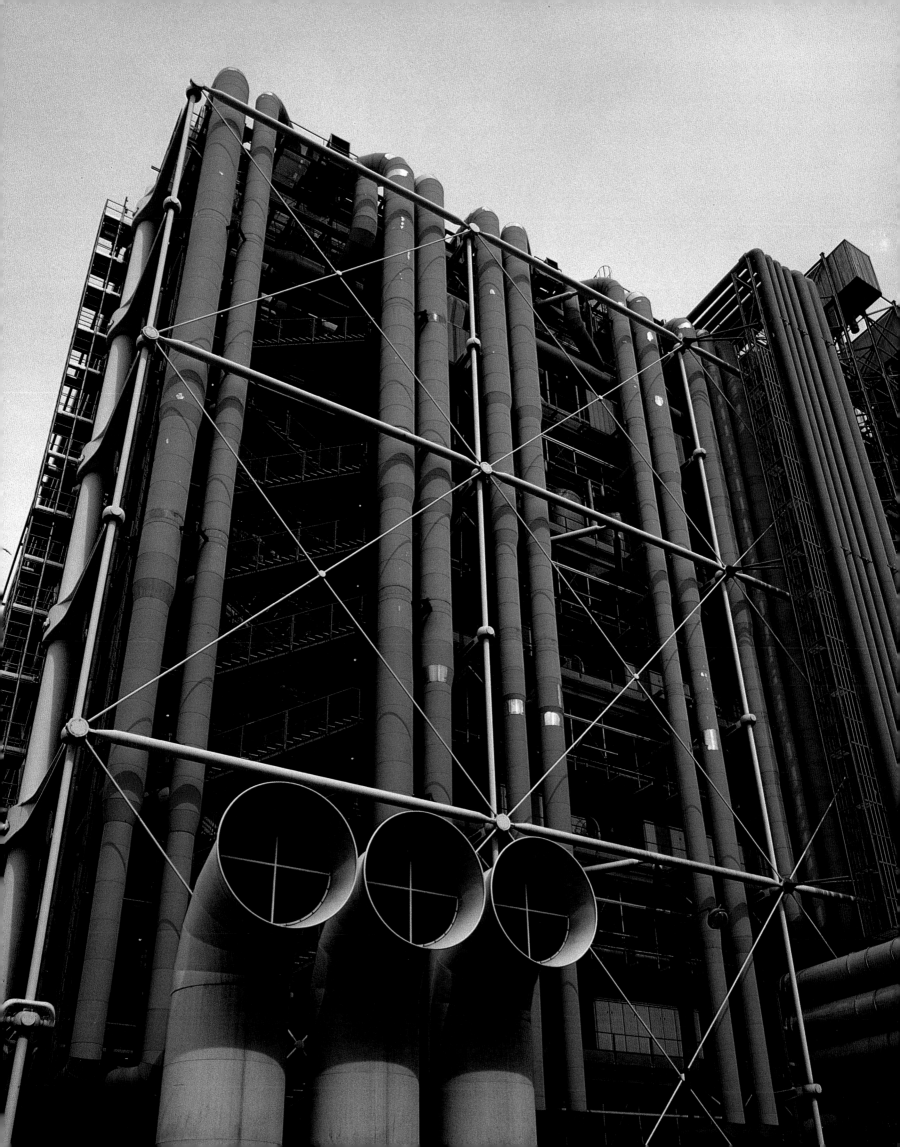

THE NEW YORK FIVE

The leading advocates of Modern design during the 1970s were influenced by Bauhaus styles of the 1920s and by Le Corbusier's purism. Known as the New York Five when their early work was popularized in the 1972 publication *Five Architects*, they included Richard Meier, Charles Gwathmey, Michael Graves, Peter Eisenman, and John Hejduk.

Meier's use of violin curves and ocean-liner railings, which took the principles of Le Corbusier's style to an extreme, influenced the direction design was taking in the 1970s. In the late 1970s, Meier designed a reading room in the Guggenheim Museum that paid homage to the museum's original architect, Frank Lloyd Wright. The furnishings for the library were designed by Meier and later produced by Knoll International.

Charles Gwathmey incorporated Le Corbusier's use of large-scale cylinders, angles, and open plans in shingled houses that architectural historian Vincent Scully has described as an adaptation of the International Style of Le Corbusier to the New England vernacular.

At the end of the 1970s, Gwathmey designed furnishings for production, as well as residences, commercial buildings, and interiors. He went into partnership in 1971 with Robert Siegel, and together they produced furniture and carpet designs that reiterated Corbusian themes and motifs.

Michael Graves, the most innovative and publicly known of the New York Five, came into prominence with a highly decorative architectural language that stressed allusions, historical reference, and spatial complexity. Because of his militant rejection of the purist forms of Modernism, Graves was a major influence on interior design in the 1970s, first through his symbolic use of colors and later through the Classical ornamentation of his architecture, furniture, and housewares.

Peter Eisenman is considered the most radical and theoretical of the New York Five. An integral part of the conceptual stage of his buildings involves architectural criticism and theory. In the 1960s, he developed a theory of architecture antithetical to most Modernist theory. The architect is more interested in exploring the inherent nature of architecture than in designing specific projects.[32]

GWATHMEY SIEGEL:
GWATHMEY SIEGEL COLLECTION

The office furnishings that Gwathmey Siegel have designed for Knoll International reflect the architect's use of simple, modern designs coupled with elegant woods and clean lines to provide an atmosphere of sophistication.

MICHAEL GRAVES:

TEAKETTLE, 1985, **SUGAR
BOWL & CREAMER**, 1988
STAINLESS STEEL

The now-famous Graves
teakettle first appeared
on the market in 1985.
As Graves explains: "The
kettle is designed to
have the character that
one might find in a
traditional kitchen. It
does not try either to be
overly sophisticated or
to play on prosaic or
utilitarian shapes. It
establishes its playful
character by its
decoration and its
simple massing (three-
dimensional form)." The
slate blue handle grip,
the dark red knobs, the
cheerful whistling bird,
plus the raised stainless
steel dots all act as
coloration and formal
decoration for the simple
conical shape of the
kettle itself.

In 1988, Graves
created a sugar bowl
and creamer set to
complement the
teakettle. In keeping
with the whimsical,
Post-Modern design of
the teakettle, Graves has
incorporated the same
playful combination of
shape, coloring, and
decoration into the
design of the sugar bowl
and creamer set.

Eisenman has adapted the International Style to what he calls "cardboard architecture." Le Corbusier's pure, rectilinear Modernist work from the 1920 and 1930s has greatly influenced the development of his style. Eisenman's buildings, white or white and gray with the addition, more recently, of limited primary colors, have the feeling of cardboard models. This results not only from their gray color but also, more importantly, from the suppression of structural detailing, the uniform texture of the walls, and the shallow interior space.[33]

As Director of the Institute for Architecture and Urban Studies in New York City, Eisenman founded the institute's journal, *Oppositions*, in 1973, to encourage architectural theory and criticism. He continues to play a major role in architectural education.

John Hejduk is, like Eisenman, more concerned with conceptual architecture, Structuralism, and teaching. He has held the position of Dean of the School of Architecture at Cooper Union in New York City for the past two decades. The majority of Hejduk's work is highly theoretical, involving investigations into the nature of architecture, and has been realized only on paper. His most highly acclaimed completed project is the renovation of the Foundation Building at Cooper Union, originally built in 1853 in the Italianate style. Hejduk's project provides a powerful contrast between the old and the new.

Architect Robert A. M. Stern was, with Charles Jencks, a vociferous spokesman for Post-Modernism within the framework of his architecture and as a critic and historian for his generation. His work from the 1970s incorporated spaces derivative of Le Corbusier, Robert Venturi, and Art Deco. Diagonals, layers of screens, and both flat-paneled and curving walls were included in his interiors, which were illuminated by Aalto-like skylights over fireplaces, over unexpected setbacks of ceiling, and from side ports.[34] All of Stern's buildings were decorated with architectural elements drawn from a variety of historical styles.

Stern has also designed accompanying furnishings and housewares that reflected the Post-Modern concern for the treatment of interiors and the consideration of the uses and users of space.

Many architects of the 1970s continued to refine the Miesian idiom of the 1960s. The work of architect/designer Charles Pfister came into prominence during the latter half of the decade when he created a tubular metal chair for the offices of fashion designer Halston. This same chair was reproduced by the Metropolitan Furniture Company. Pfister then designed a line of radius corner tables for Knoll International.

Architect/designer Warren Platner also produced sophisticated designs in the late Modern style, including the 1976 interior designs for the Windows on the World restaurant atop the World Trade Center in New York. Platner has stated that "the reason for architecture is interiors." His elegant interior design for the Grill restaurant in the TWA Terminal at Kennedy Airport in New York was, according to C. Ray Smith, "an enrichment of the building's sculptural forms with heady colors and textures."

The pluralism that began in the 1960s continued throughout the 1970s. Modernism yielded to a variety of design directions, many of which adopted past styles reinterpreted to suit contemporary needs. Nevertheless, Modernism continued to have its own group of loyal followers and promoters. The designs of Eileen Gray, Robert Mallet-Stevens, and other first-generation Modernists such as Le Corbusier, Mies van der Rohe, and Marcel Breuer are still produced by such manufacturers as Knoll International and Herman Miller, which continue to encourage a fourth generation of Modernist furniture designers.

THE NEW YORK FIVE AND BEYOND

A combination of radical innovation and historical appropriation is the hallmark of Post-Modernism in general and the New York Five in particular. Humor and color began to take the place of the austere ideal of "good design" in the domestic objects of the 1970s.

MICHAEL GRAVES:
BIG DRIPPER FILTER COFFEE POT
PORCELAIN

When asked if there was something special he would like to design for Swid Powell, the architect confessed that yes, as a matter of fact, there was. He enjoys drip coffee, but the available drip coffee makers lacked the aesthetics he felt they should have. And so, according to Swid Powell, the *Big Dripper* was born.

MICHAEL GRAVES
PEPPER MILL, 1988
STAINLESS STEEL WITH RED AND BLUE POLYAMIDE
5 1/4"

The pepper mill rises from a gently flaring bottom to a cylinder topped by two polyamide "wings." The circumference is punctuated by five rows of holes that remove the guesswork from the time to refill by allowing the user to see through the clear inner lining.

ROBERT VENTURI AND DENISE SCOTT BROWN:
EMPIRE CHAIR, 1984
LAMINATE OR WOOD VENEER FACE
24 1/4" X 23 3/8" X 32 1/2"
A playful form meets a serious function in Venturi and Scott Brown's 1984 chair.

TIGERMAN-MCCURRY:
TEA POT, SUGAR BOWL, CREAMER, AND TRAY; COOKIE JAR; SALT & PEPPER SHAKERS
PORCELAIN

Tigerman-McCurry's coffee and tea service is a lighthearted design in the shape of a midwestern farm compound. The cookie jar and salt and pepper shakers continue in the same humorous vein, the cookie jar resembling a silo-like structure, while the salt and pepper shakers, halves of screws.

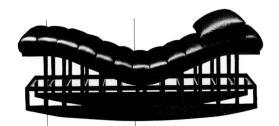

THE RICHARD MEIER COLLECTION: TABLE, CHAIR, CHAISE, 1982

For this series which Meier designed for Knoll International, the architect's clean, Modernist lines predominate. The chaise, with its simple flowing line and gridlike base structure, is reminiscent of the furniture from the Wiener Werkstätte.

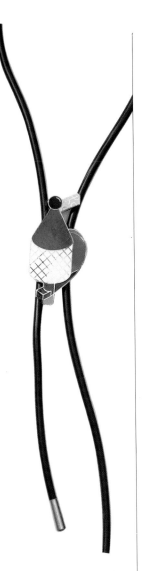

RICHARD MEIER:
CANDLESTICK
SILVER

The austere yet elegant styling of Meier's candlestick reflects the impact of the Weiner Werkstätte on his approach to Modernism.

The chairs were designed to fit the exact scale of the table; both the chair arms and the table are 27 1/2 inches high.

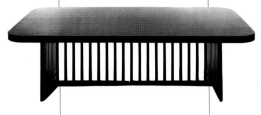

In the table the strong verticals of the base, combined with the vast panorama of the large top, create a dramatic and beautiful image.

RICHARD MEIER:
EARRINGS AND BOLO TIE
ENAMEL AND SILVER

This inexpensive jewelry was designed to reflect the architect's interest in simple, elegant shapes and gridlike patterns.

ITALIAN DESIGN

During the 1960s, Italian design witnessed the birth of an innovative language of forms. Italian furniture designers of the period created products whose forms and functions interacted with the environment. Brightly colored, disposable, and semidisposable household and industrial materials such as plastics were being manufactured and used in stacking, folding, collapsible, and inflatable forms. The open-minded and experimental climate of Italy in the 1960s helped to bring the work of Italian designers into international prominence that has continued into the 1990s.

As Kathryn Hiesinger points out in her book *Design Since 1945*, the Italian success in adapting new materials and processes to commercial furniture production in the 1960s was and remains due to the small scale of the industry. As an outgrowth of the traditional family-owned craft shops staffed with skilled artisans, the industry was able to take risks in developing products that were discouraged elsewhere by high engineering costs.

Heisinger goes on to point out that the close relationship of the Italian designer to the manufacturer and the artisan in these small shops encouraged the development of personal, expressive styles. These included brightly colored but highly rational essays in the new plastic materials; Pop or idiosyncratically shaped objects rich in symbolic meaning; and multifunctional objects suitable to flexible modes of arrangement. If good taste had been called into question in the late 1950s, it returned with a vengeance in Italian design in the mid-1960s, albeit transformed by bright colors and unusual shapes and making assertive, dramatic, and sometimes ironic statements.

VICO MAGISTRETTI:

SINBAD, 1981

GAE AULENTI:

JUMBO COFFEE TABLE,

1965

44 1/2" X 44 1/2" X 15"

The base and top of the coffee table are made from marble, with a polished finish on the marble cluster legs. The marble is coated with transparent polyester to help prevent stains.

NEW MATERIALS
AND MASS PRODUCTION

B y the mid-1950s, the plastics manufacturer Kartell had initiated a series of collaborations with several leading architect/ designers, including Gae Aulenti, Joe Colombo, Ettore Sottsass, and Marco Zanuso. The company grew large enough to encompass a number of different divisions, all emphasizing design in addition to research and technological experimentation.

Internationally known for exploiting the aesthetic and formal qualities unique to plastic, Kartell continued to grow, reflecting the emergence of Italian design as an international force and the importance of Milan as a major center for design innovation.

In 1964, the Kartell manufacturing company initiated the first structural use of polyethylene in furniture design: a child's chair by architect/designers Marco Zanuso and Richard Sapper. The following year, the first all-plastic chairs to be made by injection molding were designed by Joe Colombo.

Responsible for many innovative furnishing designs for mass production in the 1950s, Zanuso has stated: "It was in the artisan's shop that the greatest integration of capability, communication, creativity, and production was ever attained. . . . Among the many and far-reaching effects of the industrial revolution—effects which continue to define our lives today both as individuals and collectively as a society—is the separation in time and space of the act of design from the art of production.

"The result is that both the industrially produced object and the process leading to its definition and design acquire an ever-greater degree of complexity. This becomes true to the point that no single person can be said to have complete grasp of every aspect of the design process. This very important phenomenon means that in response to the complex nature of the structure of the object and the various contributions of specialized working groups, the role of the designer becomes increasingly concerned with the integration of these various components and the management and control of the interactions among them."

The 1960s and 1970s saw the expansion of Italian industrial firms, many of which hired noted architect/designers to help boost sales of mass-produced products. Firms such as

MARCO ZANUSO:
CELESTINA, 1971
STAINLESS STEEL WITH
UPHOLSTERED STEEL AND
BACK 30 1/2"

This chair represents the designer's personal interpretation of the traditional folding chair updated using a steel frame that comes in a variety of colors including burnished or fire lacquered black, anthracite, pearl-white, red, or light blue. The upholstery for the seat and back includes colored cowhide in black, brown, natural, white or light gray.

MARIO BELLINI:

LE TENTAZIONI, 1977

This chair and loveseats
contain steel frames on
wooden bases and
incorporate polyurethane
foam and polyester
padding. The architect
designed the pieces to
be upholstered in a
variety of fabrics as well
as two types of leather,
including a special thick
leather. All are fixed to
the frames by elastic
webbing.

Arteluce, Artemide, Brionvega, Fiat, Kartell, Olivetti, and Sambonet developed working relationships with leading designers and also enhanced their reputations by sponsoring national and international design awards.[35]

Arteluce, founded by Gino Sarfatti, and Flos helped to establish the reputation of modern Italian lighting. Sambonet produced kitchen equipment and utensils. Furniture manufacturers such as Cassina and Techno became known for designs that were both serviceable and stylish.

The Olivetti Company is another Italian manufacturer that in the 1950s shifted its emphasis to technology and innovative design and styling. Olivetti also worked closely with noted architect/designers Mario Bellini and Ettore Sottsass. In 1959, Sottsass designed the DE700 data entry machine after careful analysis of ergonomic and anthropometric data.

In the 1960s, many of the same designers prominent in the 1950s promoted through their work ideas of "anti-design" and "radical design." Their use of eccentric, often humorous styles aimed to shock consumers into consciously thinking about the design of a product. These radical designers were influenced by Pop Art of the 1960s in England and the United States.

Architect/designer Ettore Sottsass emerged as the leader of the radical design movement. In 1966, he founded two experimental design studios, Archizoom and Superstudio, in Florence.

Later, as a member of the Alchymia design studio, founded in 1976 by Allessandro Mendini, Sottsass and his colleagues Alessandro Guerriero, Andrea Branzi, and Michele de Lucchi created a new style in furniture and object design. The Alchymia style was characterized by bright, playful colors and lively contrasts, laminates printed with patterns resembling magnified noodles, and logic-defying forms such as sloping shelves, and asymmetrical chairs and tables.[36]

In 1972, the Museum of Modern Art in New York held "Italy: The New Domestic Landscape," an exhibition that introduced to Post-Modernists in the United States the work of Italian designers of the 1960s. Italian architect/designer Emilio Ambasz, who had taught at Carnegie-Mellon University in Pittsburgh and in Ulm, Germany, was the curator of design responsible for the exhibition and accompanying catalogue. He wrote in the introduction: "The emergence of Italy during the

last decade as the dominant force in consumer-product design has influenced the work of every other European country and is now having its effect in the United States. The outcome of this burst of vitality among Italian designers is not simply a series of stylistic variations of product design. Many designers are expanding their traditional concern for the aesthetic of the object to embrace also a concern for the aesthetic of the uses to which the object will be put."

Several different design approaches existing simultaneously in Italy were presented in MOMA's exhibition. These included what Ambasz called "Conformists," the designers who worked closely with Italian manufacturers to develop furniture, light fittings, and home and office equipment for mass production. Also represented were the antidesign radicals who provided thought-provoking designs involving satire, whimsy, and combinations of bright colors.

The Memphis Design studio was also founded in Milan by Sottsass, in 1980. Nathalie du Pasquier, George Snowden, Andrea Branzi, Michele de Lucchi, and Peter Shire worked in the studio, which within five years became a major international influence on design. The Memphis furnishings were innovative products made from wood or chipboard, either painted or faced with patterned laminates, metal, ceramic, and glass, or combinations of dissimilar materials. The odd, flamboyant shapes reflected the influence of American Pop and Post-Modernism. As historian Kathryn Hiesinger notes in *Design Since 1945*, "Memphis designers do not deny functionality but look at it with eyes wide open, more as anthropologists than as marketing specialists. Functionality, therefore, involves not only a respect for certain ergonomic rules or for profitability, but a respect for a cultural vision, a public necessity, a historical thrust."

Although Memphis designers use industrial materials and their style is popular internationally, the products are expensive and produced in limited editions by traditional craft shops. The work of Memphis has, however, spawned similar styles and philosophies promoting a language of forms that openly discourage the principles of early Functionalism.

Sottsass has stated: "The qualities of good design are

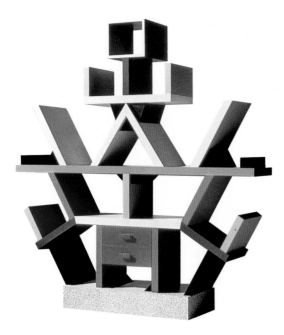

ETTORE SOTTSASS:

CARLETON, 1981
WOOD WITH PLASTIC
LAMINATE
77" X 74 3/4" X 15 1/2"

A room divider/
bookshelf composed of
an eclectic assemblage
of slabs, boxes, drawers,
and diagonals, Carleton
exemplifies the
dynamism of Memphis.

**PHOTOGRAPH OF
MARCO ZANINI,
ETTORE SOTTSASS, AND
ALDO CIBLIC**
MEMBERS OF MEMPHIS

Ettore Sottsass founded
the radical design group
Memphis, mockingly
named in reference to
the ancient egyptian city
and to the American
rock-and-roll capital.
Memphis has designed
furnishings and table-
ware for over forty years,
and its irreverent style is
a major force in design.

RICHARD SAPPER:
**COFFEE AND TEA
SERVICES**, 1983

Produced in stainless
steel by Alessi Company,
Sapper's designs reflect
the architect's use of
dramatically simple
shapes combined with
the richly expressive use
of different metal
finishes.

exactly the ones that don't endure but follow the changes of
history, the changes of the anthropological state of things, and,
among them, the changes of technology. In design what endures
is man's curiosity toward existence and the drive to give a
metaphoric image to it.

"If a society plans obsolescence, the only possible enduring
design is one that deals with that obsolescence, a design that
comes to terms with it, maybe accelerating it, maybe confronting
it, maybe ironizing it, maybe getting along with it. The only
design that does not endure is the one that in such a society
looks for metaphysics, looks for absolute, for eternity.

"The so-called antidesign movement pushed the idea that
design does not end with the product put in production by
industry but starts from that moment."

Through the 1980s, Italian design continued to occupy the
forefront of innovation. Every September, Milan hosts the
annual Milan Furniture Fair, which has become the undisputed
mecca for members of the international design community.

MASSIMO MOROZZI:
TANGRAM

Seven similar
components may be
used in various
configurations of shapes
and sizes. Available in a
variety of colors, each
component can also be
supplied individually. An
extra white or black
marble top that fits on
the wooden top of
TANGRAM 1 and a
wooden chess-board top
for TANGRAM 6 are also
available.

A sudden proliferation of new materials released a whole new wave of design in Italy in the sixties. Bright colors and playful forms gave domestic objects a new Pop aesthetic, and Italian designers quickly rose to international prominence on the basis of this new look.

ETTORE SOTTSASS:

WESTSIDE LOUNGE SEATING, 1987

16" X 35" X 31"

This chair exemplifies the Memphis style, known for its furnishings made in odd shapes and brilliant colors.

JOE COLOMBO:

BIRILLO, 1971

29 1/2"

FIBERGLASS BASE WITH A STAINLESS STEEL SUPPORTING STEM AND UPHOLSTERED SEAT AND BACK

This bar stool won the gold medal at the M.I.A. International Exhibition in 1972 and is in the permanent collection of the Kunstgewerbe Museum, Zurich, Switzerland. The designer considered this " . . . a seat that is like a person, projected as a way of life for the house and the bar . . . it is based on technologies and materials of the future."

GAE AULENTI:

FOUNTAIN PEN, 1988

18 KARAT GOLD PLATE

This pen possesses a perfect finish and is fabricated of the purest metal. Each pen has been specially created for fine, medium, or bold writing. Signed with the Louis Vuitton monogram, the pens are considered "precious travel instruments."

MARIO BELLINI:

CAB

Bellini's design required an enamelled steel frame. Leather upholstery was then zippered over the frame and over a seat padded with polyurethane.

GIO PONTI:
SUPERLEGGERA

Gio Ponti's "superleggera" chair reflects the straight-backed severity of Wiener Werkstätte designs updated with bold colors and surprising upholstery. The frame is made from ashwood and comes in black, white, red, or green with seats available in India cane, gray twisted fiber, foam rubber padding, and removable fabric or leather upholstery.

PAOLO DEGANELLO:
TORSO

Deganello's armchairs and sofas come with round table tops that can be affixed to their backs.

GAE AULENTI:
**LOUIS VUITTON I
WATCH**,
1988

The watch "designed for the true traveler." It displays other time zones as well as the traveler's current time and current phases of the moon. The case is handcrafted from a single piece of 18 karat gold.

ACHILLE CASTIGLIONE:
GIBIGIANA 41, 1981
HALOGEN LAMP WITH RED,
WHITE, ANTHRACITE

VICO MAGISTRETTI:
SINBAD

These pieces have removable upholstery, placed as a cover over a padded base of black lacquered beechwood. The upholstery cover is made of durable materials including thick hide, piqué, or wool, all trimmed with grosgrain, contrasting colors. The cover is attached to the padded frame by two hooks. An adhesive strip and two special clips near the back edges hold it securely.

TOTAL DESIGN TODAY

For more than a decade, architects have produced buildings, interiors, furnishings, and decorative and utilitarian objects reflecting the pluralism of the 1960s and 1970s.

The sources for their work are as diverse as Russian Constructivism, Art Deco, design motifs of the 1950s, and the grid patterns of traditional Japanese architecture and turn-of-the-century Viennese design. Other contemporary directions incorporated the ongoing influence of Pop Art and the mannered ornamentation of Post-Modernism. Designers continue to create furnishings influenced by the modular designs of the 1940s and 1950s.

Because of the interest in historicism and the concern for preservation, architects and designers from all camps prefer to recycle existing structures. Found objects are reused in new and unusual ways in building, interior, and product design.

Noted Post-Modern masters such as Michael Graves, Robert Venturi, Richard Meier, and Robert A. M. Stern have extended their spheres of influence to the design of housewares, furnishings, and jewelry. A wide variety of design changes can be seen in the Art Deco revivalism of Helmut Jahn, the Surrealism of James Wines and the SITE group, the sober historicism of Cesar Pelli, and the brightly colored, Latin-influenced Post-Modernism of Arquitectonica.

Several theories exist about architects' reemergent penchant for designing furnishings and products. One explanation is simply economics. American architects have learned what Europeans have known for years: designing furnishings and products is both challenging and lucrative. Once a building is completed, the profits end. A designer of furniture continues to collect royalties for as long as the product is sold.

Designing small-scale works gives architects significantly more immediate gratification than designing a building. A piece of furniture or an object can often be produced in six weeks. Furthermore, the demand for furniture and objects is steadier than the need for buildings.

JIM MURRAY AND PAUL
VON RINGELHEIM:
CANOPY CHAIR, 1986
MAPLE, ALUMINUM, PAINT
24" X 20" X 55"

Creating small-scale works also provides architects with many of the creative, mechanical, and contextual challenges posed by planning a block of large-scale buildings, but without the risk.

Small-scale works by architects are often characterized by a historical approach. Trained in art and architectural history, architects are well equipped to apply this knowledge to product and furnishing design. They have proved themselves capable of designing almost anything, from highly distinctive interiors to individualistic objects—rugs, linens, tableware, housewares, lighting, fabrics, jewelry—which together can create a total environment.

Today's total designers advocate mass production. Their furniture and objects are often distinguished by a refreshing use of existing materials and techniques or by a desire to challenge traditional industrial processes and aesthetics.

This new generation of architect/designers has continued the practice of product design as past generations have, and with the enthusiastic reception that their products have received from the general public, this legacy of total design will continue for generations to come.

KALLE FAUSET:
UNTITLED, 1986
MADRONE BURL, PURPLE
HEART, PAU AMARILLO,
EBONIZED WALNUT
30" X 26" X 30"

**SUNARHAUSERMAN
SHOWROOM, HOUSTON**
C. 1984

Gehry's longstanding interest in the design of buildings as collections of discrete objects and his deeply held conviction about the sculptural possibilities of architecture made the architect the perfect choice to design the showroom of the newly merged corporation of SunarHauserman. In order to exhibit the company's collections of objects in a way that would make them work together and, at the same time, retain their individual identities and strengths, Gehry created a village landscape.

Gehry's village had pathways that directed the movement of people within designed spaces leading to and around its structures. The furniture is placed alongside the pathways and in clearings. One looks inside the structures and through doors and windows to see other products organized for work. The architect's intent is to allow the product to be discovered and the showroom to unfold as one moves through it.

GAETANO PESCE:
TRAMONTO
A NEW YORK

This whimsical variation on modular furniture reveals the humorous innovation characteristic of contemporary Italian design.

ARATA ISOZAKI:

**HAUSERMAN,INC.
SHOWROOM, CHICAGO
MERCHANDISE MART**

Isozaki's SunarHauserman showroom exemplifies the architect's inspired integration of eastern feeling and western form. The showroom's three spatial divisions symbolize past, present, and future. Past is bounded by square colonnades, present, dominated by a barrel-vaulted nave with a series of crossings that lead to the third space, future. It is expressed as a starry black volume created with SunarHauserman walls and glass. Colors in the showroom progress from lavender pink, and green to puple-gray to a final dark, sparkling translucence.

The conference room of the showroom provides the setting for Isozaki's chair and table designs. These are beautifully proportioned ash pieces. The sensual curve of the chair back has been wryly patterned after the profile of Marilyn Monroe.

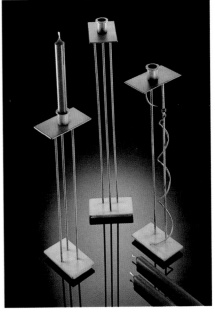

STEPHEN HOLL:

CANDLESTICKS

PATINATED BRONZE

Holl's patinated bronze
candlesticks signal his
love of fine materials
and craftsmanship.

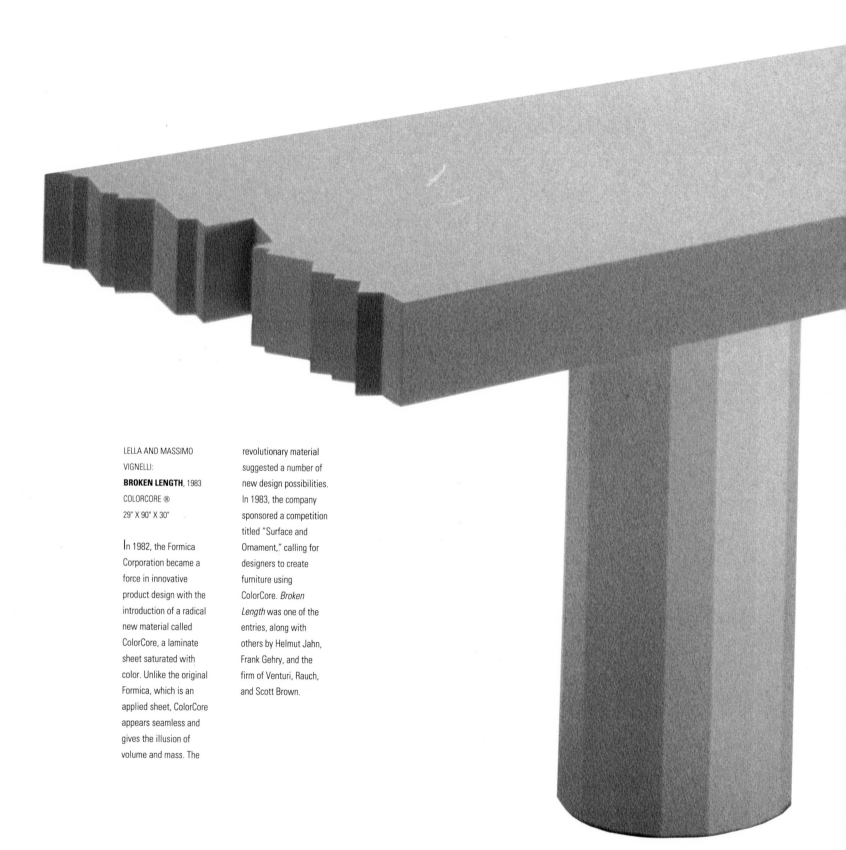

LELLA AND MASSIMO
VIGNELLI:

BROKEN LENGTH, 1983
COLORCORE ®
29" X 90" X 30"

In 1982, the Formica
Corporation became a
force in innovative
product design with the
introduction of a radical
new material called
ColorCore, a laminate
sheet saturated with
color. Unlike the original
Formica, which is an
applied sheet, ColorCore
appears seamless and
gives the illusion of
volume and mass. The

revolutionary material
suggested a number of
new design possibilities.
In 1983, the company
sponsored a competition
titled "Surface and
Ornament," calling for
designers to create
furniture using
ColorCore. *Broken
Length* was one of the
entries, along with
others by Helmut Jahn,
Frank Gehry, and the
firm of Venturi, Rauch,
and Scott Brown.

SITE PROJECTS, INC.:
**LIGHTHOUSE/
DARKHOUSE**

This miniature
lighthouse was designed
to be auctioned for the
benefit of children's
programs at The
Lighthouse in February,
1989.

MARK MACK:

WASSERTISCH

(WATER TABLE), 1988
FABRICATED BY GARY
KAPLAN, SAN FRANCISCO
35" X 24" X 60"
FORMICA BRAND 2000X®,
METAL, ASH, BRASS
FAUCET, GLASS MIRROR.

W*assertisch*, a water
table, is furniture for
daily cleansing. This
piece is neither a
plumbing fixture nor a
vanity table: it is truly a
combination of building
science and emotion.

Wassertisch
integrates various
unrelated functions into
one design, while
remaining a piece of
furniture with standard
cabinet-grade finish.
This *Wassertisch* stands
clear of the floor and
wall so one can see
the limits of the
architecture. It is only
connected to water and
sewage systems through
transparent plastic
hoses that accentuate
the act of cleaning.

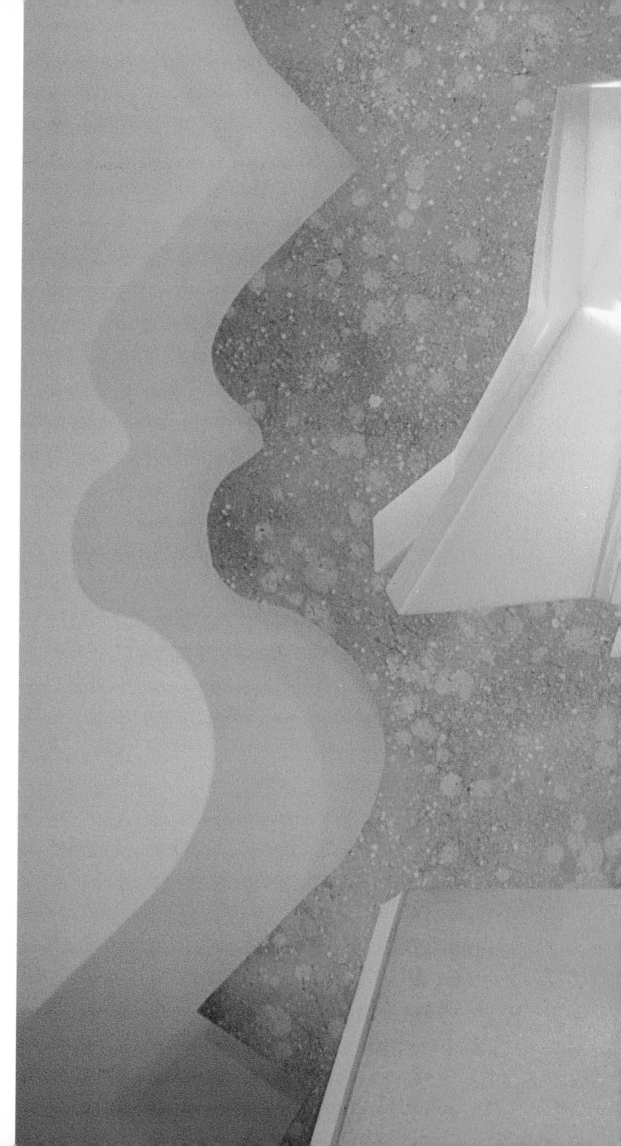

PATRICK ELIE NAGGAR:
HYPNOS SLEEP LIGHT
FABRICATED BY
ENVIRONMENTS PLUS,
CINCINNATI
5" X 5" X 16"
FORMICA 2000X ®, METAL,
LAMP

H*ypnos Sleep Light* is a
poetic design for
illumination, incense,
and dreams. A blue wing
swings back and forth
across a circular hole in
the towerlike base,
creating hypnotic
rhythms in light. As
Hypnos glows, it heats
the metallic incense/
perfume container fitted
on top.

MARK SIMON:

BREEZE

PROJECT ASSISTANT:
MARGARET WAZUKA
FABRICATED BY
PLEXABILITY LTD., NEW
YORK
FORMICA BRAND 2000X®,
ELECTRICAL.
28" OVERALL HEIGHT;
LAMPSHADE 10" AT TOP,
20" AT BOTTOM

Breeze is a light fixture
offering many pleasures.
Its solid base holds a
fragmented and
surprisingly luminous
shade. In a world
accustomed to air-
conditioning, the fixture
suggests open windows
and spring days. While it
evokes memories of old-
fashioned table lamps, it
also recalls the romance
of Cubism, when ideas
were fresh and new.
Mark Simon is an
award-winning architect
and partner at
Centerbrook Architects
and Planners in Essex,
Connecticut.

POST-MODERN PLATES

A dinner plate—the ultimate tabula rasa— is the perfect format for new design ideas. In the eighties, Post-Modernist designers used dinnerware for all kinds of experimentation. The strictures of function precluded much variation in form, but decoration and pattern were open territory.

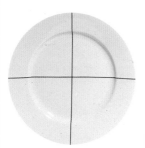

RICHARD MEIER:
SIGNATURE
PORCELAIN 12"

Meier's love of geometric forms and precise patterns is evident in this buffet plate.

STEPHEN HOLL:
PLANAR
PORCELAIN BUFFET PLATE
12"

In his interior architecture as well as in his designs for furnishings and housewares, Holl specifies exacting adherence to the art and science of architecture.

STEPHEN HOLL:
VOLUMETRIC
PORCELAIN BUFFET PLATE
12"

This porcelain buffet plate designed for Swid Powell repeats the motifs the architect employs in his work. *Planar* is a graphic foray into form; *Volumetric* is a multicolored medley of volumes.

ROBERT AND TRIX HAUSSMANN:
STRIPES
12"

This husband-and-wife team creates work notable for its range—from bank interiors to fabrics and dinnerware—and for its consistently intriguing reliance on optical illusions and trompe l'oeil.

LAURINDA SPEAR:
MIAMI BEACH
BUFFET PLATE IN
PORCELAIN 12"

Laurinda Spear has been called the Ginger Rogers of architecture, thanks to the devil-may-care flair of her firm's condominium towers in home-base Miami. Swid Powell invited the architect to do for tabletops what she has done for the South Florida skyline. The result is a sprightly colored buffet plate appropriately entitled *Miami Beach*.

ROBERT AND TRIX HAUSSMANN:
ZURICH
PORCELAIN BUFFET PLATES
12"

For Swid Powell, the Haussmanns indulged their fascination with optical illusions in a series of buffet plates.

ETTORE SOTTSASS:
MEDICI
PORCELAIN DINNERWARE
12"

This porcelain dinnerware reflects the architect's colorful, playful style.

ROBERT VENTURI:
NOTEBOOK, 1986
PORCELAIN
12"

This decorative dinnerware is reminiscent of the patterns found on the cardboard-covered school notebooks from the 1950s.

TIGERMAN-MCCURRY:
VERONA
PORCELAIN
12"

Tigerman-McCurry's humor is reflected in this playful design for a series of dinner and dessertware.

ETTORE SOTTSASS:
MADRAS
PORCELAIN
12"

This dinnerware demonstrates the architect's whimsical styling and use of bright colors.

ARATA ISOZAKI:
STREAM
PORCELAIN
12"

Arata Isozaki's porcelain buffet plate for Swid Powell reflects the architect's subtle formality of design.

ROBERT VENTURI:
VEGAS
PORCELAIN
12"

As this plate illustrates, instead of Minimalism, Venturi advocates "messy vitality," an inclusive approach to design that looks to popular culture, historical movements, and local context as points of reference.

PAGE 105: CHARLES AND RAY EAMES, **LOUNGE AND OTTOMAN**. PHOTOGRAPH COURTESY OF HERMAN MILLER, INC.

PAGE 106: **PHOTOGRAPH OF GEORGE NELSON**. PHOTOGRAPH COURTESY OF HERMAN MILLER, INC.

PAGE 107: EERO SAARINEN, **TULIP ARMCHAIR**. COURTESY OF KNOLL INTERNATIONAL LTD.

PAGE 109: CHARLES AND RAY EAMES, **STACKING, GANGING, MOLDED FIBERGLASS CHAIRS**. PHOTOGRAPH COURTESY OF HERMAN MILLER, INC.

PAGE 110: ALVAR AALTO, **TEA TROLLEY**. COURTESY OF ARTEK

PAGE 111: ALVAR AALTO, **EASY CHAIR**. COURTESY OF ARTEK

PAGE 113: GUNNAR ASPLUND, **GOTEBORG,1**. COURTESY OF ATELIER INTERNATIONAL LTD.

PAGE 114: JOE COLOMBO, **STACKING CHAIR**, COURTESY OF KARTELL USA

PAGE 117: MARCO ZANUSO: **MAGGIOLINA**. COURTESY OF AREACON, INC.

PAGE 118: **PHOTOGRAPH OF ALEXANDER GIRARD**. PHOTOGRAPH COURTESY OF HERMAN MILLER, INC.

PAGE 121: **INSTALLATION BY ALEXANDER GIRARD**. PHOTOGRAPH BY CHARLES EAMES, COURTESY OF HERMAN MILLER, INC.

PAGE 123: FRANK LLOYD WRIGHT, **THE SOLOMON R. GUGGENHEIM MUSEUM**. COURTESY OF THE FRANK LLOYD WRIGHT ARCHIVES

THE AGE OF PLURALISM

PAGE 127: RICHARD MEIER, **CHAIR**. COURTESY OF KNOLL INTERNATIONAL

PAGE 129: PAOLO DEGANELLO AND GILBERTO CORRETTI, **ARCHIZOOM SEATING SYSTEM**. COURTESY OF ATELIER INTERNATIONAL

PAGE 130: LUDWIG MIES VAN DER ROHE AND PHILIP JOHNSON, **SEAGRAM BUILDING**. PHOTOGRAPH COURTESY OF JOSEPH E. SEAGRAM AND SONS

PAGE 134: WARREN PLATNER, **THE PLATNER COLLECTION**. COURTESY KNOLL INTERNATIONAL

PAGE 136: VENTURI, RAUCH AND SCOTT BROWN, **TREE HOUSE: NEW CHILDREN'S ZOO**. PHOTOGRAPHS © MATT WARGO

PAGE 138: RICHARD ROGERS AND RENZO PIANO, **CENTRE GEORGES POMPIDOU**. PHOTOGRAPH © 1990 ROBERTO SONCIN GEROMETTA/PHOTO 20-20

PAGE 140: GWATHMEY SIEGEL, **GWATHMEY SIEGEL COLLECTION**. COURTESY OF KNOLL INTERNATIONAL

PAGE 143: MICHAEL GRAVES, **TEAKETTLE, SUGAR BOWL & CREAMER**. COURTESY OF ALESSI

PAGE 144: WARREN PLATNER, **LOUNGE CHAIR**. COURTESY KNOLL INTERNATIONAL

PAGE 146: MICHAEL GRAVES, **BIG AND LITTLE DRIPPER FILTER COFFEE POT, CREAMER & SUGAR BOWL**. COURTESY OF SWID POWELL

PAGE 146: MICHAEL GRAVES, **PEPPER MILL**. COURTESY OF ALESSI

PAGE 146: TIGERMAN-MCCURRY, **TEA POT, SUGAR BOWL, CREAMER AND TRAY; COOKIE JAR; SALT & PEPPER SHAKERS**. COURTESY OF SWID POWELL

PAGE 146: ROBERT VENTURI AND DENISE SCOTT BROWN, **EMPIRE CHAIR**. PHOTOGRAPH © JENNIFER LEVY.

PAGE 147: RICHARD MEIER, **THE RICHARD MEIER COLLECTION: CHAISE, CHAIR, TABLE**. COURTESY OF KNOLL INTERNATIONAL

PAGE 147: RICHARD MEIER, **CANDLESTICK**. COURTESY OF SWID POWELL

PAGE 147: RICHARD MEIER, **EARRINGS AND BOLO TIE**. COURTESY OF ACME STUDIOS

ITALIAN DESIGN

PAGE 151 AND 167: VICO MAGISTRETTI, **SINBAD**. COURTESY OF CASSINA

PAGE 153: GAE AULENTI, **JUMBO COFFEE TABLE**. COURTESY OF KNOLL INTERNATIONAL

PAGE 154: RICHARD SAPPER, **TIZIO**. COURTESY OF ARTEMIDE, INC.

PAGE 155: MARCO ZANUSO, **CELESTINA**. COURTESY OF AREACON, INC.

PAGE 156: MARIO BELLINI, **LE TENTAZIONI**. COURTESY OF CASSINA

PAGE 158: ETTORE SOTTSASS, **MANDARIN ARM CHAIR**. COURTESY OF KNOLL INTERNATIONAL

PAGE 160: ETTORE SOTTSASS, **CARLETON**, COURTESY OF SOTTSASS ASSOCIATI, MILAN, ITALY

PAGE 161: **PHOTOGRAPH OF MARCO ZANINI, ETTORE SOTTSASS, AND ALDO CIBLIC**, COURTESY OF SOTTSASS ASSOCIATI, MILAN, ITALY

PAGE 163: RICHARD SAPPER, **COFFEE AND TEA SERVICES**. COURTESY OF ALESSI

PAGE 164: MASSIMO MOROZZI, **TANGRAM**. COURTESY OF CASSINA

PAGE 166: MARIO BELLINI, **CAB**. COURTESY OF CASSINA

PAGE 166: JOE COLOMBO: **BIRILLO**. COURTESY OF AREACON, INC.

PAGE 166: ETTORE SOTTSASS, **WESTSIDE LOUNGE SEATING**. COURTESY OF SOTTSASS ASSOCIATI, MILAN, ITALY

PAGE 166: GAE AULENTI, **FOUNTAIN PEN**. COURTESY OF LOUIS VUITTON IN 1977 FOR KNOLL INTERNATIONAL

PAGE 167: GIO PONTI, **SUPERLEGGERA**. COURTESY OF CASSINA

PAGE 167: PAOLO DEGANELLO, **TORSO**. COURTESY OF CASSINA

PAGE 167: GAE AULENTI, **LOUIS VUITTON I WATCH**. COURTESY OF LOUIS VUITTON

PAGE 167: ACHILLE CASTIGLIONE, **GIBIGIANA 41**. COURTESY OF FLOS INCORPORATED

TOTAL DESIGN TODAY

PAGE 171: JIM MURRAY AND PAUL VON RINGELHEIM, **CANOPY CHAIR**. PHOTOGRAPH © JENNIFER LÉVY

PAGE 173: KALLE FAUSET, **UNTITLED**, PHOTOGRAPH © JENNIFER LÉVY

PAGE 175: FRANK GEHRY, **SUNARHAUSERMAN SHOWROOM, HOUSTON**. COURTESY OF SUNARHAUSERMAN

PAGE 177: GAETANO PESCE, **TRAMONTO A NEW YORK**. COURTESY OF CASSINA, S.P.A.

PAGE 178: ARATA ISOZAKI, **HAUSERMAN, INC. SHOWROOM, CHICAGO MERCHANDISE MART**. COURTESY OF SUNARHAUSERMAN

PAGE 179: STEPHEN HOLL, **CANDLESTICKS**. COURTESY OF SWID POWELL

PAGE 180: LELLA AND MASSIMO VIGNELLI, **BROKEN LENGTH**. CRAFTED BY DAVID GEISE, FORMICA CORPORATION DESIGN CENTER, CINCINNATI. COURTESY OF THE FORMICA CORPORATION

PAGE 182: SITE PROJECTS, INC., **LIGHTHOUSE/ DARKHOUSE**. COURTESY OF SITE PROJECTS INC.

PAGE 183: MARK MACK, **WASSERTISCH**. COURTESY OF THE FORMICA CORPORATION

PAGE 184: PATRICK ELIE NAGGAR, **HYPNOS SLEEP LIGHT**. COURTESY OF THE FORMICA CORPORATION

PAGE 185: MARK SIMON, **BREEZE**. COURTESY OF THE FORMICA CORPORATION

PAGE 186: ROBERT AND TRIX HAUSSMAN, **ZURICH**. COURTESY OF SWID POWELL

PAGE 186: RICHARD MEIER, **SIGNATURE**. COURTESY OF SWID POWELL

PAGE 186: LAURINDA SPEAR, **MIAMI BEACH**. COURTESY OF SWID POWELL

PAGE 186: STEPHEN HOLL: **PLANAR**. COURTESY OF SWID POWELL

PAGE 186: STEPHEN HOLL, **VOLUMETRIC**. COURTESY OF SWID POWELL

PAGE 186: ROBERT AND TRIX HAUSSMANN, **STRIPES**. COURTESY OF SWID POWELL.

PAGE 187: ARATA ISOZAKI, **STREAM**. COURTESY OF SWID POWELL

PAGE 187: ROBERT VENTURI, **NOTEBOOK**. COURTESY OF SWID POWELL

PAGE 187: TIGERMAN-MCCURRY, **VERONA**. COURTESY OF SWID POWELL

PAGE 187: ETTORE SOTTSASS, **MEDICI**. COURTESY OF SWID POWELL

PAGE 187: ROBERT VENTURI, **VEGAS**. COURTESY OF SWID POWELL

PAGE 187: ETTORE SOTTSASS, **MADRAS**. COURTESY OF SWID POWELL

FOOTNOTES:

1. Wendy Kaplan, *"The Art That Is Life": The Arts & Crafts Movement in America, 1875-1920* (Boston: The Museum of Fine Arts, 1987), 54.

2. Penny Sparke, Felice Hodges, Emma Dent Coad, and Anne Stone, *Design Source Book* (London: QED Publishing Ltd., 1986), 28.

3. Ibid., 45.

4. Wendy Kaplan, *"The Art That Is Life,"* 108.

5. Penny Sparke, *Design in Context* (London: Quarto Publishing Inc., 1987), 42-55.

6. *Nineteenth Century Furniture: Innovation, Revival and Reform*, Introduction by Mary Jean Madigan (New York: Billboard Publications, 1982), 64.

7. Wendy Kaplan, *"The Art That Is Life,"* 52.

8. Robert Judson Clark, editor, *The Arts and Crafts Movement in America 1876-1916* (Princeton: Princeton University Press, 1982), 59.

9. Penny Sparke, *Design in Context*, 83.

10. Ibid., 84.

11. Penny Sparke et al., *Design Source Book*, 95.

12. C. Ray Smith, *Interior Design in 20th-Century America: A History* (New York: Harper & Row Publishers, 1987), 81.

13. Michael Collins, *Towards Post-Modernism* (Boston: New York Graphic Society, 1987), 66.

14. Penny Sparke et al., *Design Source Book*, 141.

15. Penny Sparke, *Design in Context*, 87.

16. Stephen Bayley, Philippe Garner, and Deyan Sudjic, *Twentieth-Century Style & Design*, 117.

17. *Design Since 1945*, organized by Kathryn B. Hiesinger (Philadelphia: The Philadelphia Museum of Art, 1983), x-xi.

18. Stephen Bayley et al., *Twentieth-Century Style & Design*, 171.

19. C. Ray Smith, *Interior Design in 20th-Century America*, 176-77.

20. Ibid., 180.

21. Penny Sparke et al., *Design Source Book*, 149.

22. Ibid., 150.

23. Stephen Bayley et al., *Twentieth-Century Style & Design*, 175.

24 *Design Since 1945*, vx.

25. C. Ray Smith, *Interior Design in 20th-Century America*, 204.

26. Penny Sparke, *Design in Context*, 211.

27. Penny Sparke et al., 165.

28. Penny Sparke, *Design in Context*, 212.

29. Michael Collins, *Towards Post-Modernism*, 120.

30. C. Ray Smith, *Interior Design in 20th-Century America*, 274.

31. David Gebhard and Deborah Nevins, *200 Years of Architectural Drawing* (New York: The Whitney Library of Design, 1977), 275.

32. Ibid., 246.

33. Ibid., 247.

34. C. Ray Smith, *Interior Design in 20th-Century America*, 300-01.

35. Stephen Bayley et al., *Twentieth-Century Style & Design*, 260-64.

36. Ibid., 260-64.